Jewel Changi Airport

With contributions by:

Liew Mun Leong
Chairman, Changi Airport Group

Lee Seow Hiang
CEO, Changi Airport Group

Moshe Safdie
Lead Design Architect, Safdie Architects

Jaron Lubin, Charu Kokate
Principals, Safdie Architects

Adam Greenspan
Lead Landscape Architect, PWP Landscape Architecture

Craig Schwitter, Cristobal Correa
Lead Engineers, BuroHappold

Patrick Bellew, Meredith Davey, Henry Woon
Environmental Designers, Atelier Ten

Martin C. Pedersen
Architecture Critic

Sam Lubell
Editor

images Publishing

Jewel Changi Airport

Published in Australia in 2020 by
The Images Publishing Group Pty Ltd
ABN 89 059 734 431

Offices

Melbourne
6 Bastow Place
Mulgrave, Victoria 3170
Australia
Tel: +61 3 9561 5544

New York
6 West 18th Street 4B
New York City, NY 10011
United States
Tel: +1 212 645 1111

Shanghai
6F, Building C, 838 Guangji Road
Hongkou District, Shanghai 200434
China
Tel: +86 021 31260822

books@imagespublishing.com
www.imagespublishing.com

The Images Publishing Group Reference Number: 1540

NATIONAL LIBRARY OF AUSTRALIA

A catalogue record for this book is available from the National Library of Australia

Title: Jewel Changi Airport // Safdie Architects
ISBN: 9781864708509

Edited by Sam Lubell and Jaron Lubin

Book design by Michael Gericke and Matt McInerney

Printed on 157gsm GoldEast matte art paper by Everbest Printing Investment Limited, in Hong Kong/China

This title was commissioned in IMAGES' Melbourne office and produced as follows: *Editorial* Georgia (Gina) Tsarouhas, *Production* Nicole Boehringer

IMAGES has included on its website a page for special notices in relation to this and its other publications. Please visit www.imagespublishing.com

Contents

The Vision

Introduction

Sam Lubell
Editor

What is wonder?

The Oxford English Dictionary calls it "a feeling of amazement and admiration, caused by something beautiful, remarkable, or unfamiliar." Merriam-Webster calls it "a cause of astonishment or admiration." American Heritage calls it "the emotion aroused by something awe-inspiring, astounding, or suprising."

For me, wonder moves and elevates our spirit and transcends everyday existence. It leaves a mark on our psyche and our soul.

Of course the definition of wonder is subjective. But for all of us it is something we feel in our bones when we experience it. Unfortunately it is something we rarely sense in air travel today.

There was once a time when commercial aviation—at least on the surface—was a wondrous thing, celebrating the sheer amazement of shooting into the sky and soaring at unheard of speeds on metal wings. Travelers wore their best suits and dresses; meals were served on porcelain and eaten with silverware; the best airports embodied the speed, elegance, and audacity of this experience. Now it's generally a soul-sucking exercise involving hassle, banality, and impersonal practicality.

Jewel Changi Airport returns wonder to air travel. It again lifts our beings and creates a new paradigm for how we think about journey, and about the public spaces related to it. It does this by deftly merging architecture, urbanism, public space, landscape, greenery, transit, and retail in a new way. It's not a building. It's not a garden. It's a complex hybrid, a layering of spaces and experiences and dimensions.

Such a leap into new territory exemplifies what separates wonder from mere awe or amazement, and separates Jewel from other projects, be they airports or not. A wonder like Jewel provides a new experience that still feels familiar. It returns us to childhood, when fresh adventures and a sense of curiosity and surprise so often evoked wonder.

This is so important in a time when so little feels new. When we can see so much digitally, but experience so little that is profound "In Real Life."

Author Rachel Carson, who sparked the modern environmental movement with her book *Silent Spring*, addressed this breach more than half a century ago:

> "A child's world is fresh and new and beautiful, full of wonder and excitement. It is our misfortune that for most of us that clear-eyed vision, that true instinct for what is beautiful and awe-inspiring, is dimmed and even lost before we reach adulthood.

> If I had influence with the good fairy who is supposed to preside over the christening of all children, I should ask that her gift to each child in the world be a sense of wonder so indestructible that it would last throughout life, as an unfailing antidote against the boredom and disenchantment of later years, the sterile preoccupation with things that are artificial, the alienation from the sources of our strength."

With its deep layering of awe-inspiring natural, jaw-dropping man-made, and all-encompassing community, Jewel taps into these inherent sources of strength in a holistic, authentic way. It fulfills our deep, biological need to interact with a far greater world, both human and non-human. As Edward O. Wilson, author of *The Biophilia Hypothesis* put it, "our urge to affiliate with other forms of life."

"We are natural beings and there is a strong bond between humans and other species. As long as we deny this bond or do things that work against it, we will not find mental or emotional balance," writes Clemens Arvay, author of *The Biophilia Effect*.

In a world that is urbanizing, and balkanizing, faster than ever, we have an especially acute need for interaction and harmony with something larger than ourselves: a greater community of people and other life forms. Moreover, we long to experience the health advantages of being in nature's sights, sounds, sensations, and smells—from clean air to stress relief to physical recuperation to immune boosting. As we move further inward, further from our natural roots, we need to feel physically part of the greater tapestry of being. We need to leave our man-made bubble and be reminded that as animals, we belong in nature, our home.

To create something so different, so profound, requires another prerequisite for a true wonder: pushing beyond what has been done before, and beyond what is comfortable. In Jewel's case this required a level of sophistication, coordination, and *risk* that was a marvel in itself. Its concept was at once perfectly simple and astonishingly complex. In execution, the impossibly multifaceted interaction of its parts and its players more resembled a symphony than a typical work hierarchy or organizational chart.

And like most wonders, Jewel—a new gateway for a place with a deep identity as a modern crossroads for the world—perfectly encapsulates the best of its age and the best of its place. Virtually every technology employed to make it a reality is at the front edge of its field. No location on earth has tempered the effects of density and urbanization as effectively as Singapore, a city-state of 5.6 million people locked in the space of 720 square kilometers. Jewel reflects and brings to light the country's exhaustive, holistic efforts to use sophisticated planning, green regulations, iconic architecture, and constant reinvention to enhance livability and carve out a name for itself.

So we celebrate Jewel's crystallization of these efforts and this place, and its re-elevation of air travel and of public space, through brave, groundbreaking, multidimensional design that has created something new. In her book *The Mystery of the Hanging Garden of Babylon*, author Stephanie Dalley describes the criteria for a world wonder: the project needs to be "magnificent in conception, spectacular in engineering, and brilliant in artistry." More than 2,500 years after the Hanging Gardens, Jewel fulfills these lofty standards. But beyond that it fulfills a simpler standard: you simply don't want to leave. When was the last time you felt that way in an airport?

T1
Jewel Drop-off
Jewel Car Park
MERGE
SLOW
HEIGHT LIMIT
HEIGHT LIMIT

Jewel Changi Airport is situated just behind Changi's iconic Airport Control Tower

Liew Mun Leong
Changi Airport Group

Chairman

I recently accompanied Chinese Ambassador Hong Xiaoyong on a visit to Jewel. The moment he saw it, he turned to his embassy colleagues and said in Mandarin, "This is innovation in Singapore!" Then he diplomatically repeated that to me in English.

I responded that Jewel is indeed a bold innovation in ideas and technology, informing him that it was originally an open-air carpark built about 40 years ago. I was the engineer in charge of building that carpark. It has now been converted into a high-value, multifunctional commercial asset with extended airport functions, shopping, restaurants, airport hotel, recreational facilities and attractions, plus 2,500 parking spaces.

Jewel is a clear demonstration of our continued efforts to ensure that Changi Airport remains a leading international air hub. I have been involved with the building of Changi since its early phases in 1975, but Jewel is truly one of the highlights of my professional career.

Its birth began at least nine years ago. Changi was critically short of parking lots at Terminal 1, which was hemmed in by Terminal 2 and Terminal 3. Expansion was possible only at the open-air carpark in front of Terminal 1, but we rejected the obvious solution of simply building a multistory carpark there.

Changi Airport Group Chief Executive Lee Seow Hiang came to me one day with the idea of constructing a commercial building with additional parking spaces on the site. The proposed building could be integrated with an expanded Terminal 1 and open the possibility for us to reimagine what airport infrastructure could be.

Frankly, at the time I was skeptical that the idea could work financially. But I left it to Mr. Lee and his team to innovate and develop his new "dream." Eventually, a bold and highly imaginative glass dome was conceptualized and designed by world-renowned architect Moshe Safdie.

There was one key strategic goal throughout: to upgrade and maintain the attractiveness of Changi Airport as an international air hub by entertaining and providing stopover passengers with more "pleasurable transit time." We also wanted to better serve growing passenger segments such as those who travel to Singapore to connect to cruises and ferries. And we wanted Jewel to be a space for all Singaporeans to enjoy bonding with family and friends.

Of Grit and Gumption

Executing Jewel did not happen without hurdles. Besides financial viability, we had to address queries from various agencies on the need for another mall at Changi Airport. Would it cannibalize sales from the nearby shops and shopping malls? Aggravate the problem of a shortage of retail workers? Cause traffic jams at the airport?

These were valid concerns, and it took three years to persuade all the relevant stakeholders. Finally, Prime Minister Lee Hsien Loong signaled his endorsement after we presented the project to the Cabinet at the Istana. His response was encouraging: we would do it as a "leap of faith." That year, the concept of Jewel was introduced to Singaporeans at the National Day Rally, and there was palpable excitement. Four-and-a-half years of hard work followed to construct a complex project that Mr. Safdie rated as 9 out of 10 in terms of its technical difficulty.

Setting a New Benchmark for the Aviation Industry

On April 17, 2019 the day of Jewel's opening, there were families of all races and ages, including children and the elderly, some arriving in wheelchairs. They were smiling, excited, and fascinated with the extraordinary project that stood before them. Some looked bewildered, and marveled that such a feature could be built in Singapore.

I could almost hear them thinking proudly: "Singapore can build this and we own it!"

Internationally, Jewel has also gained much attention, receiving overwhelmingly positive press coverage.

Recently, a gentleman with two children stopped me at the fifth floor of Jewel to congratulate us on its success. He said that he had been there five times over the last two months to enjoy the facilities. Jewel has set a new benchmark in air travel, greatly strengthening Changi Airport as an international air hub and providing the public, who may not be air passengers, with an additional public space to enjoy.

Space in Singapore is very precious. I am glad we have managed to innovatively unlock the value in this open-air carpark by turning it into a Jewel. As Changi Airport Group enters a new decade, with the Changi East development beckoning, it will have to embrace the risks and challenges of an even more unpredictable aviation environment.

We may not know what success will look like in the future, but as long as our people remain deeply rooted in the values and sense of purpose that have underscored Changi Airport's achievements, we can be assured that the Singapore air hub will remain competitive and stay ahead of the game.

Terminal 1
BRITISH AIRWAYS

Lee Seow Hiang Changi Airport Group

CEO

Since its opening in 1981, Changi Airport has soared as an international air hub. Changi now serves more than 120 airlines flying to some 380 cities in about 100 countries and territories worldwide. Each week, about 7,400 flights land or depart from the airport, with more than 65.6 million passengers passing through each year. Changi has garnered close to 600 best airport awards to date.

Right from the beginning, Jewel—built on the site of what had been an open-air carpark in front of Terminal 1—was designed to help Changi adapt to the growing region and the changing world. It grew out of our need for constant reinvention and innovation. A game-changing airport development was a must.

In creating this new development, we of course believed that it needed to fulfil its practical function. But more than that we wanted it to reinvent what an airport could be. We wanted it to leave visitors with deep memories and create an iconic gateway representing Singapore to the world.

Our plans grew out of what we had already been doing at Changi. Through a strong planting program, we knew the magic horticulture brings. We were one of the first airports to offer intensive retail, and we knew that it resonated with passengers. We also knew that we wanted strong attractions that could draw people. But after all these dreams were sketched out, we needed an architectural manifestation.

When the submissions for our international competition came in it was apparent that the CapitaLand and Safdie team understood our dreams and were able to translate them into physical form. Their submission was beautiful, but beyond that it fulfilled the purpose of the land. Safdie unlocked its potential. It was natural, seamless, and authentic. It wasn't a vanity project or about winning awards. It was about looking at our customers and fulfilling their needs. We were already doing bits of each of these elements in a small way, and we were testing them out with our customers. But not on this scale. Not in one place. It was all our dreams in one place.

Moshe Safdie's breakthrough idea was to elevate our requirement for a novel horticultural design by creating a paradise garden. "A garden like no other," as he put it. His proposal united a marketplace, activity center, and paradise garden in one integrated destination. It would be a new urban typology, combining commerce and nature. A mixed-use development like Jewel would allow us to serve different customer segments—both locals and visitors to Singapore alike—giving everyone a spectacular reason to come.

Jewel Changi Airport opened on April 17, 2019. The countless drafts on paper finally came to life as Singaporeans and travelers arrived to marvel at what Jewel had to offer. Millions have visited since. Jewel

Changi Airport Control Tower, Terminal 1, and the open-air carpark that would one day become the site for Jewel Changi Airport

"Where we are now is well beyond what our imaginations could have ever fathomed."

stands now as a sparkling gemstone in the crown of Changi Airport, a signature destination that will enhance Singapore's tourism appeal and add to Changi's appeal as one of the world's leading air hubs.

This is a place that rewards you in many ways. You can bounce on the nets like a young kid again. Or you can look up and see the control tower from a new angle. There is quiet commerce. There is bustling commerce. Jewel is fundamentally an inclusive place that provides a deep sense of community.

One of the most beautiful pictures I have in my mind is when you walk into the Forest Valley and you see that mix of travelers, locals, old and young, enjoying the place. That's what completed the project for me.

Airports around the world are coming to the same conclusion: that there's so much more untapped potential to their facilities. Where we are now is well beyond what our imagination could have ever fathomed.

We hope Jewel will help change what travel means. That it will help make all airports a little more human, fun, and yes, enjoyable. That it will create countless memorable experiences and change travel for the better. We look forward to welcoming the world here.

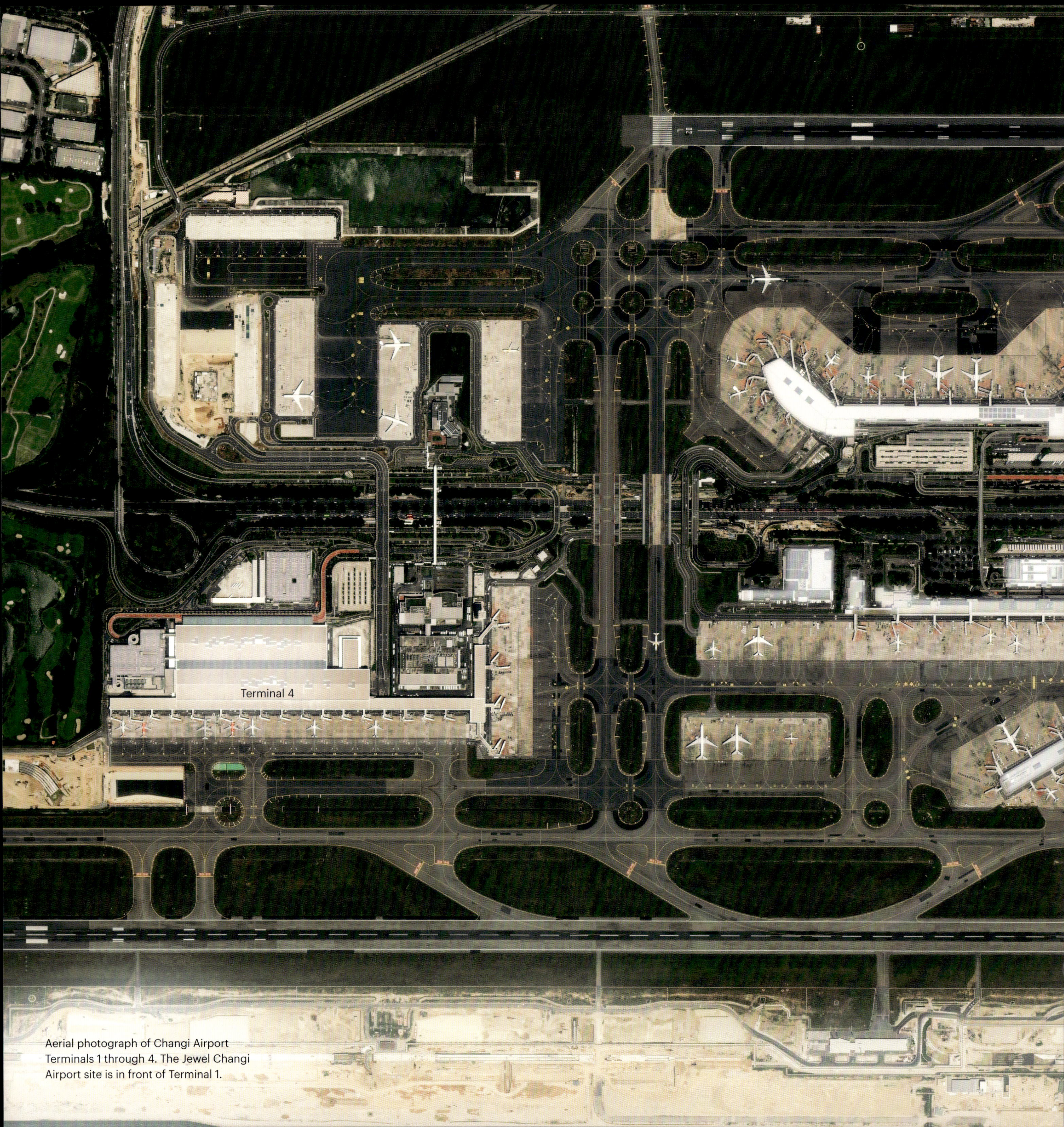

Aerial photograph of Changi Airport Terminals 1 through 4. The Jewel Changi Airport site is in front of Terminal 1.

Terminal 3
Jewel
Changi
Airport
Terminal 1
Airport Boulevard
Terminal 2

The Design Concept

Safdie Architects' rendering of Jewel, situated between Terminals 1, 2, and 3

Moshe Safdie
Safdie Architects

Lead Design Architect

Like many airports, Singapore's Changi Airport has grown and evolved incrementally, adding much-needed new terminals in 1981, 1990, and 2008. By 2012, pressure had again mounted on the airport, prompting officials to consider an addition south of Terminal 1, on the site of a parking area between the terminal and the airport's Air Traffic Control Tower. They also started to consider building something new; something Changi and other airports had never possessed.

Until recently, airports have focused primarily on airport operations and the direct needs of passengers. In the last few years, a new component has been added: concentrating retail in passengers' path to generate income. This strategy, generated largely by duty free outlets, expanded to a full offering of shops, from fashion to electronics.

While these developments generally occurred on the airside of terminals, the landside was also transforming. Airport cities, which incorporated hotels, office spaces, regional transportation centers, and warehousing and logistics facilities, were increasingly evolving into urban centers, serving both passengers and the urban region at-large.

This evolution must have been on the minds of Changi officials, as well as the government of Singapore, when they conceived the program for Jewel. The facility, serving passengers, airport employees, transit passengers, and the citizens of Singapore on both the air and land sides, would offer a much wider program than any airport facility before. According to their brief, Jewel would have to be a destination and a major attraction. Retail would therefore be augmented by entertainment, and a wide range of food and beverage options, and, as the program stated, a major attraction. Changi's leadership recognized that to make Jewel the destination it had hoped for, it had to attract passengers to choose Singapore as its endpoint over competitive airports in the region. They launched a competition—which has become customary for all major Singapore projects on public land— for developers and architects worldwide to help determine what this attraction should be.

The design competition was launched in September 2012. Each developer-architect team would propose a profitable, financially self-sustaining plan to conceive what the complex should be and what attractions it might incorporate. The winning developer would enter into a joint venture with Changi, sharing in the cost and income generated by the project. Thus, fantasies and creative ideas had to be balanced with compelling financial models. We already had an established relationship with our partners, CapitaLand, with three major projects under construction: Sky Habitat, a residential

Early design sketches illustrate the geometry and organization of the building, and the genesis of the Forest Valley and Rain Vortex

complex in central Singapore; LuOne, a mixed-use development in Shanghai; and Raffles City Chaotianmen, a 10-million-square-foot mixed-use development on the most significant site in Chongqing. We embarked with the CapitaLand team to evolve a design as well as a concept.

It is in the nature of competitions that they get the adrenaline going. They energize the process for search and invention. While it was clear that each of the shortlisted developers would bring a wealth of experience and know-how to the design of the requested 90,000 square meters of retail, it was our focus on the whole experience that would lead to our project's selection.

To us, wide-ranging attractions too often focus on the creation of fantasy worlds, a model that began with Disneyland and has proliferated around the world. These include the make-believe re-creation of historic settings, story themes, and nature, like dinosaurs, aquariums, and desert gardens. In our brainstorming with CapitaLand, many such possibilities were discussed, including a dinosaur theme park, which would appeal to the young and perhaps their parents.

I tended to be somewhat skeptical. Many themed presentations don't appeal to a particular sector of the population at all. Moreover, once you've experienced them, there is not often the motivation to return; few encourage multiple visits. Anything that would appeal mostly to adults or mostly to children seemed inappropriate for the airport setting. We would be serving, also, the traveling population, which, by definition, includes the full range of ages, income groups, and interests.

Something more universal, more timeless, was needed. It was also important to consider both the residents of Singapore and airline passengers. Travel is stressful. People emerge in the terminal either before or after a major journey. Much of the traffic in Singapore includes long-haul flights, often transferring between other long-haul flights. It seemed appropriate to find an attraction that would have a calming and uplifting effect; one that would lend repose to the journey.

Thus, the idea of a great garden slowly emerged; a garden like no other interior garden experienced before. It would be a place of commerce and a place of nature. It would be a ying and yang of the marketplace, the bazaar, and the shopping arcade, all juxtaposed with a great urban park. Except that this park would be enclosed and protected from the noise and heat outside; truly an oasis.

Jewel would be a great garden in a city that, from its inception by Prime Minister Lee Kuan Yew, has been dubbed the "City in a Garden,"

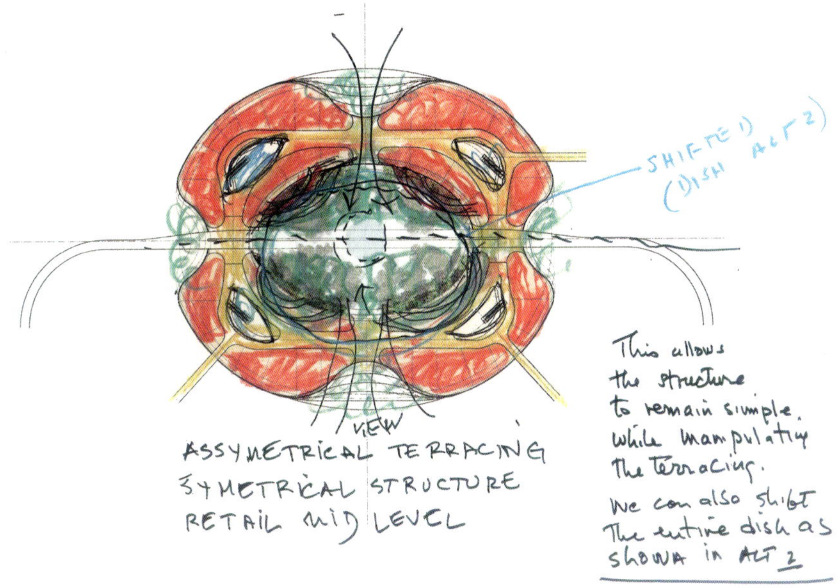

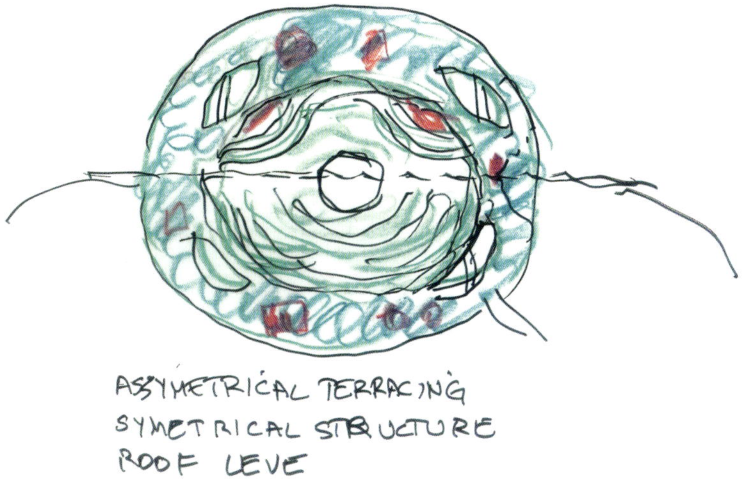

Early sketches illustrate the gardens (green) and retail areas (red)

and has evolved into one of the greenest cities in the world. It already possessed a world-famous Botanic Garden and, more recently, Gardens by the Bay, which offers climate-controlled tropical and subtropical gardens for the enjoyment of residents and visitors. Could we create yet another natural attraction?

As the idea began to catch on, we sketched away with early concepts that would transform the abstract concept into a physical proposal. Given the rectangular shape of the site, its flow at one end to Terminal 1, and its less direct connection to Terminals 2 and 3 (with a train bisecting the site), we began to develop an elliptical loop of shopping arcades surrounding the site and connecting at three points to the other terminals. The shopping program, as well as the airport facilities, soon evolved into a five-level stacking of space. The sketches evolved into a great dome, elliptical in shape, and covering most of the site, hovering over a loop of shopping arcades, containing the great garden.

The design came to life when it evolved into a toroid—a dome that dipped inwards, like a doughnut, creating a suspended oculus in space. Such a structure, made of glass and steel, would allow sunlight to penetrate, sustaining plant life at various levels, while also bringing daylight to each and every floor. It would collect the rainfall on its vast roof and drain it toward the oculus, entering the space as a 40-meter-tall waterfall. We soon calculated that with a good Singapore rainfall, this would amount to 3,780 liters per minute—a powerful display of nature's force. The water would be collected and redeployed as one of the many green strategies to obtain maximum sustainability. As we worked, sketches soon became elaborate computer 3D constructs. Simultaneously, and seemingly instantaneously, large models representing the structure and its spaces could be studied firsthand.

As one would expect, though the structure was elliptical, the toroid proposed for the roof was symmetrical on its two axes. It soon became clear, however, that the waterfall would be coming down on the train, whose path was already fixed and constructed, passing through the center of the building. Drenching the train as it came by each time seemed extreme and improbable. We soon evolved an asymmetrical toroidal shape, shifting the vortex toward the control tower to avoid the train and resulting in a more complex, and exceedingly more beautiful series of spaces and structures. It would take us many months to resolve the geometric and structural complexity of this move, though we never ceased to enjoy its positive impact, both on the plan of the building and the space.

The abstract notion of a garden juxtaposed with a busy marketplace now became specific and real. Any doubts about the

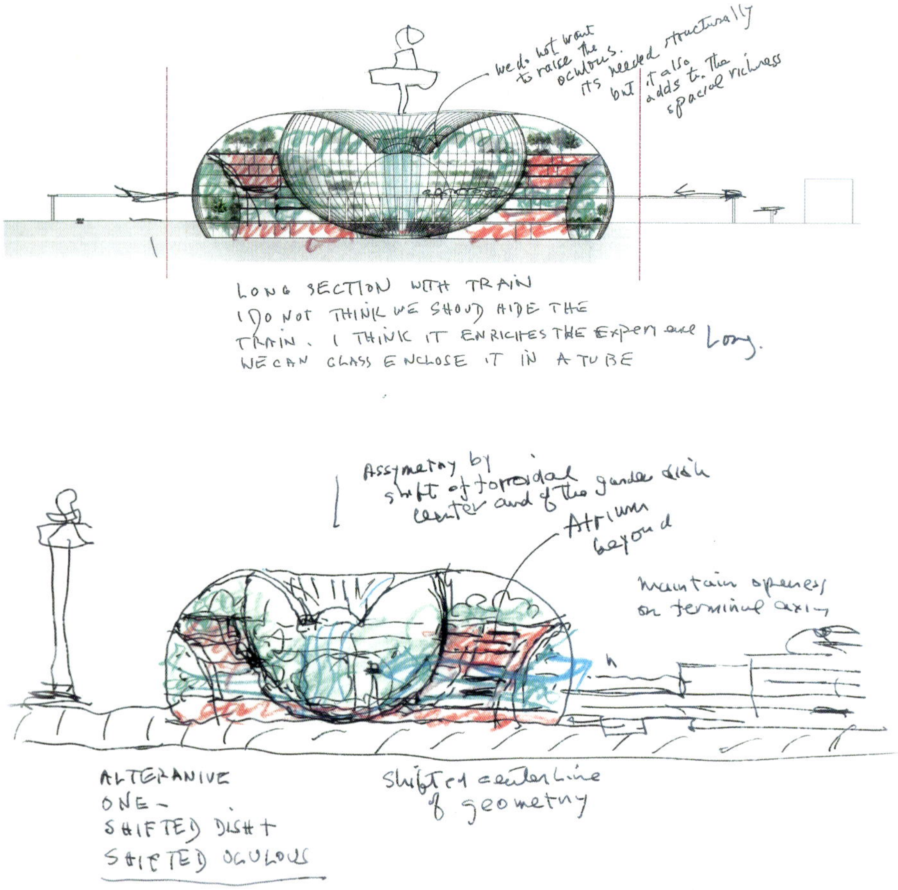

Sketches illustrate the decision to shift the center of the building's geometry north of the Changi Airport Skytrain

ability of a garden to truly become an attraction—given the many competitors in Singapore—or to be a sustained attraction for a generation or two to come, began to vanish as we examined the proposed scheme in three dimensions. The garden would ascend to a plateau where many attractions could be integrated into the landscape. Activities for young and old—event plazas, beer gardens, slides, mazes, and net walks. Then there would be the terraced gardens, descending toward the Forest Valley. This is where the flora would come into its own, with pedestrian trails extending from the plateau to the valley floor, allowing the public to explore the gardens, climbing inclines, enjoying waterfalls, and passing dramatic canyons. This would be the point of visual connection between the shopping and the gardens.

To be sure, there were heated discussions between those advocating for the gardens and those for the marketplace. Should the retail shops be able to penetrate the park from the surrounding loop, making their presence known to those experiencing the gardens? Should shop fronts and retail brands be included in the building's pastoral experience? Our recommendation was that the marketplace and the park were two contrasting experiences, and they should exist side by side, each holding their own. Therefore, no commercial activity would be present in the park, with the exception of restaurants and cafés whose dining and sitting areas could extend to overlook the park, much like a restaurant in a botanical garden enables its customers to enjoy the surrounding nature. Other than that, the visual connections would be limited to the gateways and canyons, where park and retail connect to the various terminals.

The design was submitted by CapitaLand to Changi on February 13, 2014, and together with submissions by Lendlease (with Grimshaw) and Far East Organization (with UNStudio) became the subject of intense evaluation. We know that the other attractions proposed were very much in the tradition of theme parks. One did in fact propose a dinosaur park. Architecturally, other proposals presented structures that appeared very much like a commercial mall in the center of the airport. I believe the contrast of our proposal—with the grand dome acting as the airport's new focal point and connector, drawing the terminals together in form and function—became a major consideration of selection.

Moreover, the timelessness and longevity of the garden presented a compelling argument in favor of our proposal. Jewel is different. The indoor forest contributes to humanizing this large-scale urban development. When you walk inside, the building does not seem like a structure. Instead, it seems like an organic object, possibly from outer space, almost defying gravity. You cannot quite figure out what holds the building up. I think that's what gives Jewel a lightness of being. Airports can sometimes be chaotic, stressful places. Jewel offers an alternative experience, with plenty of diversity for visitors and citizens, young and old. My hope is that people visit Jewel and feel uplifted. That Jewel shows to the world how it is possible to create a place of repose even in an airport.

After May 3, 2014, when the joint venture between Changi and CapitaLand was announced, we began the challenging process of evolving and crafting a building along with our brilliant experts in engineering, landscape, climate, structure, acoustics, and construction. It would be a process in which we would tirelessly address multiple programmatic, operational, and technical requirements, as we will outline in the chapters ahead.

1. Rain Vortex
2. Forest Valley
3. Canopy Park
4. Retail
5. Immersion Garden
6. Food hall
7. Carpark
8. IMAX Theatre
9. Coach access
10. Basement level 2
11. Level 1
12. Level 2
13. Level 3
14. Level 4
15. Level 5

Cross section illustrates the juxtaposition of Jewel's gardens and the marketplace

1
3
4
9
5
7

Safdie Architects' competition-stage rendering of the Forest Valley

The Dream Exceeded

View through the North Canyon
to the Forest Valley

Linkage bridges connect the terminal buildings to Jewel

Bridge connection from
Terminal 3 to Jewel

← JEWEL

The East Gateway Garden and entry features a hanging fern garden

The North Gateway Garden entry to Jewel features Cao Perrot's dramatic hanging art installation *Crystal Clouds*

View to Level 2 Duplex shops and North Gateway Garden. The four gateways and four canyons allow for glimpses into the gardens and provide orientation to the building.

Jewel features six levels of daylit retail

OPEN

2

Voids through Jewel's retail floor plates create a sense of light, space, and connection

Left: Changi Airport Skytrain travels through a retail gallery

Right: Escalators move visitors through several retail levels

Select restaurants and retailers feature terraces that overlook the Forest Valley

Planted canyons feature fern and palm installations, as well as vertical green walls rising 28 meters in height. The canyons serve as visual and physical connectors between the Forest Valley and retail spaces.

Left: Bamboo Grove, East Canyon

Right: Palms, West Canyon

Entry to the Forest Valley via the 38-meter-high North Canyon, which features hundreds of trees and plants. The Forest Valley is directly accessible from the Terminal 1 baggage claim.

The Rain Vortex is located at the center of the Forest Valley

BOARDING GATE

The West Trail's mist feature creates cloud-like cooling effects

Two trails meander through the Forest Valley, crossing multistory canyons and are lined with a great diversity of trees and plants

Left: North Canyon and Event Plaza at Level 5. The plaza can be cordoned off for events.

Right: A one-of-a-kind 14-meter-tall acrylic cone catches the water of the Rain Vortex, while bringing daylight to the basement levels of the building

Left: Arrival to Canopy Park at Level 5

Right: Event Plaza features a deployable sail shade system overhead

CHANGI

Canopy Park's Central Walkway runs 400 meters around Jewel's upper level, connecting an array of attractions

The glass-floored Canopy Bridge spans 50 meters over the Forest Valley

Families enjoy the Foggy Bowls attraction

BOSTON

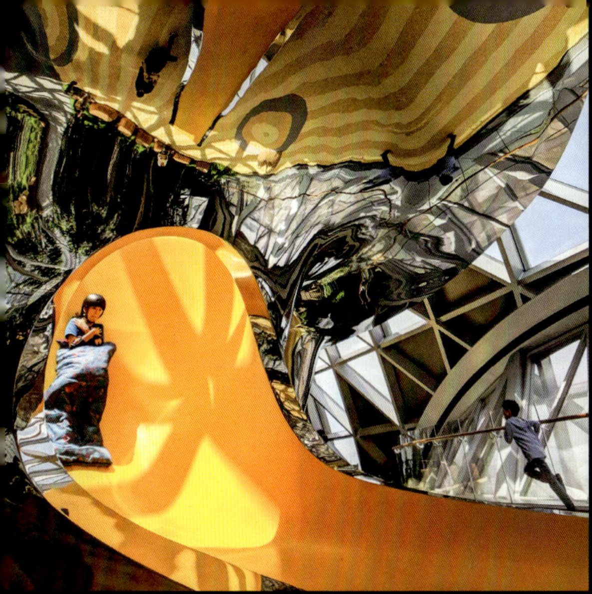

Visitors test their fortitude on the SkyWalk

The Canopy Park Central Walkway and Discovery Slides installation. The 6.5-meter-tall slides are clad with mirrored stainless steel.

Left: A water feature located at Canopy Park is the source to Cataract Falls, which cascades five stories through the Forest Valley

Right: The Rain Vortex lit up at night

Water and lighting specialist WET Design created an immersive light and sound show that projects onto the Rain Vortex at night

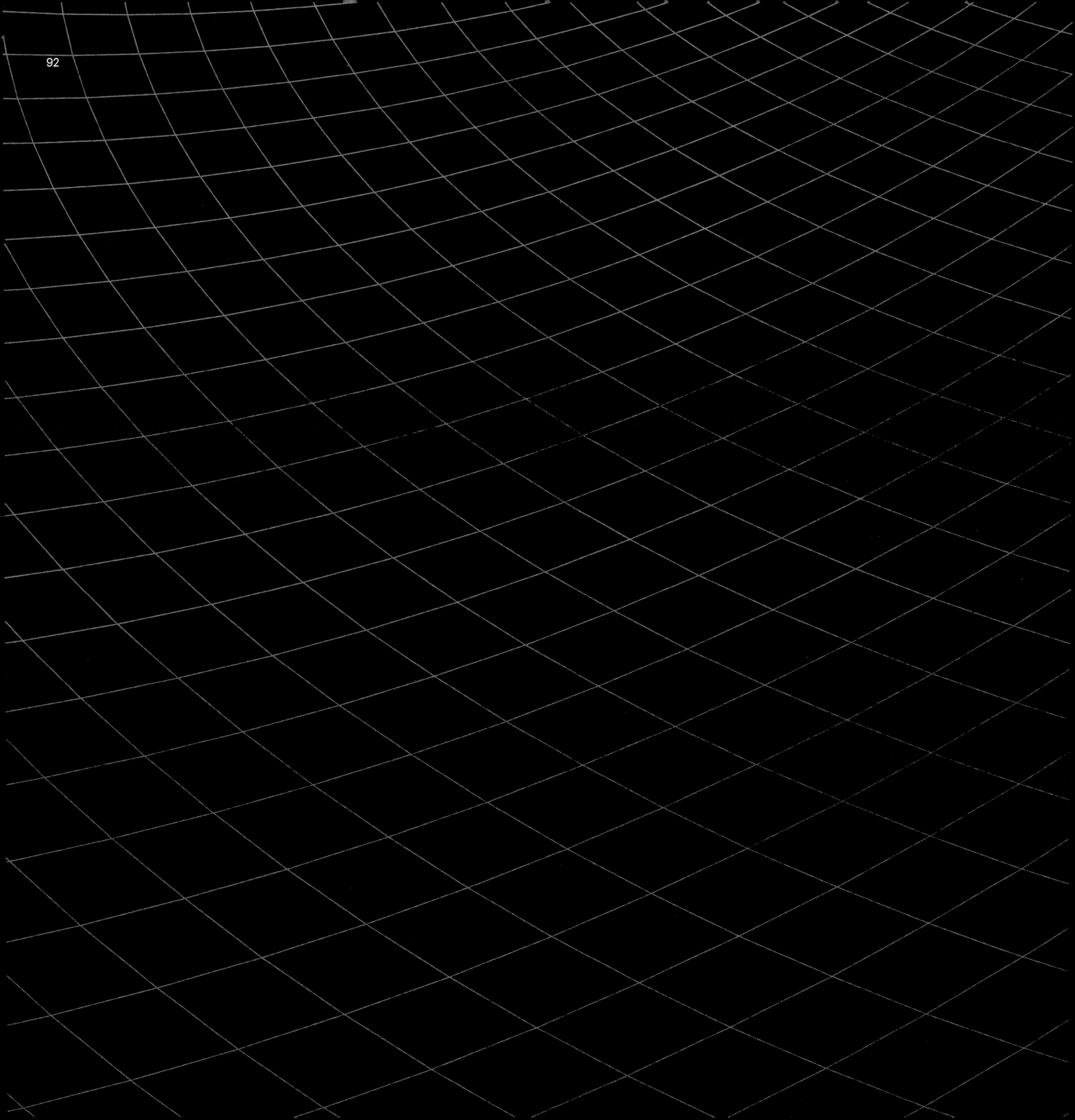

A New Public Realm

A New Public Realm

Martin C. Pedersen
Architecture Critic

For architects, there is a comforting myth surrounding the history of airports and architecture. Once upon a time, we're told, there was a "golden age" of air travel. The buildings created for that era were sleek, modern, and *fun* (a word no one associates with airports today). But a look through the relevant literature tells a different story. The glamorous *Mad Men*-era of air travel, if it existed at all, was painfully short lived. Eero Saarinen's TWA Flight Center, an undisputed masterpiece, was outdated and overwhelmed virtually the day it opened. Sadly, the same was true for most of the architecturally distinguished terminals built during that brief and shining moment. The aviation industry struggled to keep up with surging demand—a demand that has not really abated in the ensuing half century—and then quickly pivoted, trading design quality and a certain grandeur for the factory model that has prevailed ever since. Today, whatever amount of time we spend in airport terminals is imposed on us. No one without a ticket goes to the airport.

Fortunately, there is an entirely different truth in Singapore. Like any major transport hub, Changi Airport is a massive people-processing machine. It moves about 66 million travelers a year through four huge and bustling terminals with startling efficiency (and has plans to move many millions more). What takes at least 40 minutes at LAX or Kennedy or O'Hare—the physical acts of retrieving luggage, exiting the terminal, boarding a train, bus, car, or taxi, and leaving the gravitational pull of the airport, with its lines, traffic, and interminable waiting—is dispensed with in Singapore in about 20. Other airports can surely claim similar efficiencies (although exactly *zero* in the U.S. that I can think of). None can match Changi's boldest achievement: one of the most astounding new public spaces anywhere.

I had seen the images of Jewel prior to landing in Singapore, so I knew what was inside that glass-and-steel bubble located in front of the airport's iconic control tower. But looking at the building from the galloping vantage point of a moving sidewalk, slaloming through families with straggling kids, I welcome its dome-shaped, almost otherworldly form. Jewel feels like a friendly invader. (Think E.T.'s rescue ship.) At night, its round, glowing presence provides visual relief from the immense rectilinear terminals that stretch out, seemingly, as far as the eye can see. I also know that the main attraction—Changi's audacious experiment in placemaking, the urban garden—is wrapped in something a bit more prosaic: a gleaming multilevel airport mall. That is not a criticism, merely an observation: Every commercial airport in existence serves as a tool for economic development. (Singapore's special genius.)

Photo by acclaimed artist Matthew Pillsbury, shot for *The New York Times Magazine* Voyages Issue, To Points Unknown: Photographic Dispatches

9:00 10:30 10
139 9:15 9:15 11 PITTSBURGH CHICAGO
now boarding
44 10:00 10:00 8 BOSTON
15 11:10 11:10 9 CHICAGO LOS ANGELES

"It's insane," I hear a man say to his companion, in a sort of awed whisper, "but in a completely good way."

But the real surprise comes when I stroll through the mall and finally step foot inside the garden, the Forest Valley, as the architects call it. I am shocked that I am shocked! I had seen it on the web in all of its two-dimensional glory. The Rain Vortex (the world's largest indoor waterfall), the five floors of terraced trees, and the steps between them snaking to the sky. The dramatic glass-and-steel roof, the monorail slicing through the vast space like a World's Fair apparition. It's a great relief to realize that, as amazing as those images were, they still don't do the garden full *sensory* justice. They can't possibly capture the physical properties of falling water, (you can fall into a trance just looking at that), the leafy smell of the terraced forest, the faint whiff of dissolving mist, the play of sun and clouds on the roof, or the shards of sunlight shooting through cascading water. To experience this, in real time, at an airport, encased in an airport mall, 10,000 miles from home, makes me giddy. "It's insane," I hear a man say to his companion, in a sort of awed whisper, "but in a completely good way."

And yet—Singapore being Singapore—it's not at all insane. The dense city-state has a well-deserved reputation for plotting, planning, and accounting for nearly every acre of valuable land. As a result, large developments tend to be executed on swift and aggressive timelines, often in concert with supporting infrastructure. It's a coordinated approach that makes Singapore the envy of planners everywhere. And the expansion of the airport will be no different. Jewel—a partnership between Changi Airport Group and CapitaLand—is prelude to a much bigger effort. The airport recently announced plans for construction of a fifth terminal (to be designed by Heatherwick Studio, in collaboration with KPF) that will add runways and nearly double Changi's capacity. Completion is set for 2030.

Jewel will be the front door for all of this projected growth. As a quasi-public space, as a civic building, the building is a fascinating hybrid. It is both a huge retail complex and a spectacular urban park. An international hub for travel and a wildly popular local destination. A nature refuge and a front door for the world's seventh busiest airport. And baked into the economic logic of the development is Singapore's long love affair with airports. Even before Jewel exponentially upped the ante, locals have been flocking to the subterranean world of Changi for years, to eat, shop, hang out, go to the movies, and buy groceries. Planners love to talk about "airport cities," but most of the time that's still shorthand for a traditional get-in/get-out airport. Changi (along with Tokyo Narita Airport and a few others) is an anomaly: an actual "aerotropolis," heavily frequented by local residents. That history alone should ensure Jewel's economic viability for years to come.

Although the building houses nearly 54,000 square feet of retail—and that component is the project's economic reason for being—Jewel is still spatially oriented, with sightlines, signage, and interstitial spaces positioned toward its beating heart. You are always aware of the garden. You catch glimpses of it in many restaurants, where tables peek out into the forest. Some vistas provide stirring views of the Rain Vortex, but the full impact of the space isn't fully felt until you step completely inside it. And when you do, the effect is utterly altered: all vestiges of the mall tend to fall away. It is a series of spatial moves, both subtle and generous, that enhance the experience of the garden without in any way compromising the shopping around it. That kind of artful dance between the two worlds occurs all over the building.

The building itself also acts as an orienting object for the entire airport. I didn't fully understand the layout of Changi until I rode the escalator down to the second basement level (there are five), directly under Terminal 1, where the airport proper meets the glistening new amenity. Peering up through a huge expanse of glass, facing the main entrance to Jewel two floors up, I saw how the new building linked up with Terminal 1, the bus and subway lines, car and taxi pick up, connecting walkways, and the skytrain, and almost instantly understood the internal logic of the entire airport. As a result—though I did wander a lot during my visit—I was never once lost.

The garden, I soon realized after visiting at different times during the day, attracts a fluid mix of people. In the early morning, it is weary travelers who have somehow stumbled off the plane into some sort of secret garden. They appear both thrilled and perplexed (a combination I partially attribute to jet lag). As the day progresses, school children arrive and the mix begins to shift. At night, after work, when the setting sun begins to cast, the great room in a warm glow, the hourly light shows commence to a packed house spanning many generations. This feels like the beginning of a daily ritual, a Singaporean tradition. It seems beside the point to wonder whether I'm in an airport or a mall. What I'm witnessing are the daily social rhythms of a great urban park. No wonder they love it.

Airport officials estimate that between 40 and 50 million people will visit Jewel during its first year. Judging from the early crowds, those might be conservative numbers. Still, it's hard to say how the perception of this grand civic room—very much in the tradition of New York's Grand Central Station (also surrounded by stores, with an Apple store inside the hall)—will evolve over time, because it's new and still very much in its billion-selfie moment. But it will change, of course. For Singaporeans—who will have grown up in the garden, eaten in the food court downstairs, gone on dates at the movie theater—the intense sense of wonder they're experiencing now (and recording, copiously) will be replaced by something deeper: a connection to people, places, and memories; a sublime connection to nature that might be more fleeting and elusive in the future, and ultimately more important to their emotional well-being.

Whatever the future of air travel, arriving passengers years from today are unlikely to lose that initial jolt of awe upon seeing the garden for the first time. It's a sort of biophilic rollercoaster: we take in the spectacle, like children; moments later our bodies register a kind of peace. Closing the eyes amplifies the effect. We've just stepped off a plane, sealed for 12 hours in a steel tube, and been handed an unexpected gift.

That feeling of generosity is likely to deepen over time, because Moshe Safdie and his team have used as their basic tools primal elements connected to our DNA: light, water (the source of life), nature, gravity, and beauty. These will surely outlive the zeitgeist, at any moment in time. And if the great garden of Changi inspires imitators—airports from all over the world, seeing dollar signs and opportunity, in the creation of authentic public spaces—then that will have been just *one* of Jewel's great legacies. Perhaps Changi can usher in a second golden age. One centered not so much on the miracle of flight (a given today) but on the shared humanity of everyone involved.

Safdie once said that the basic idea behind Habitat 67, the project that launched his extraordinary career, was embodied in a motto: "For everyone a garden." More than a half century later, more than halfway around the world, he has provided a similar offering, lush and wonderful, to weary travelers and the people of Singapore.

EACH MOMENT
BEST FEELINGS

Realizing the Dream

CEO

The Jewel team included Singaporean and international experts working hand in hand with Changi Airport Group and CapitaLand. Full-scale mock-ups were utilized as a centerpiece of design development and design team decisions.

Choreography Matters
Safdie Architects

Jaron Lubin
Charu Kokate
Principals

A masterfully conducted piece of music transcends the mechanical reading of notes on a page, and can shift toward something more powerful—a poetic performance. As architects, proper conducting can transform the simple act of building into the act of placemaking. At Jewel Changi Airport, our role was conductor, of a project whose scale and complexity presented great challenges, but allowed us to pull off ideas that had never before been achieved.

We brought together an exceptional group with a wide range of expertise, including retail specialists, airport planners, structural and façade engineers, horticultural gurus, day-lighting experts, artists, exhibit designers, and water-feature and lighting specialists, to name a few. We also had the good fortune to work hand in hand with two exceptional clients: CapitaLand, our longtime partner, and Changi Airport Group, whose operations and service have been named by Skytrax the best in the world seven years in a row.

The key to the project was to balance the multitude of voices, interests, and functional requirements, which were often in opposition to one another. For example, the needs of people and plants are quite different from one another, and the wants of a retail marketplace are often at odds with those of a great garden. Together with our colleagues, we developed a relationship where every player had a significant role in the ensemble, and together we aimed to strike a balance in our music.

One example of this collaboration came in the shaping of the overall building form. In working with our geometry experts and engineers, we found that every millimeter of curvature change in the roof would affect the depth of all of its steel elements, which in turn would create more shadows in the garden, limiting the quantities of daylight nourishing the plantings below. This would change the planting palette altogether. No one project discipline was free from affecting another.

The Rain Vortex feature, too, was intimately connected with other aspects of the building. Its mist created a microclimate that could impact the cooling systems, so its water flows were carefully tuned by all team members to minimize splash and noise. Visits to its heroically sized full-scale mock-ups were attended not only by architects and engineers, but acoustic experts, climate specialists, and artists.

One more example of our team's unique collaboration was the Changi Airport Skytrain, which traverses the site and moves through the building. While the original design included a large glass tube enclosure, separating interior cooled spaces from exterior, we realized that this would split the garden in two. It took the cooperation

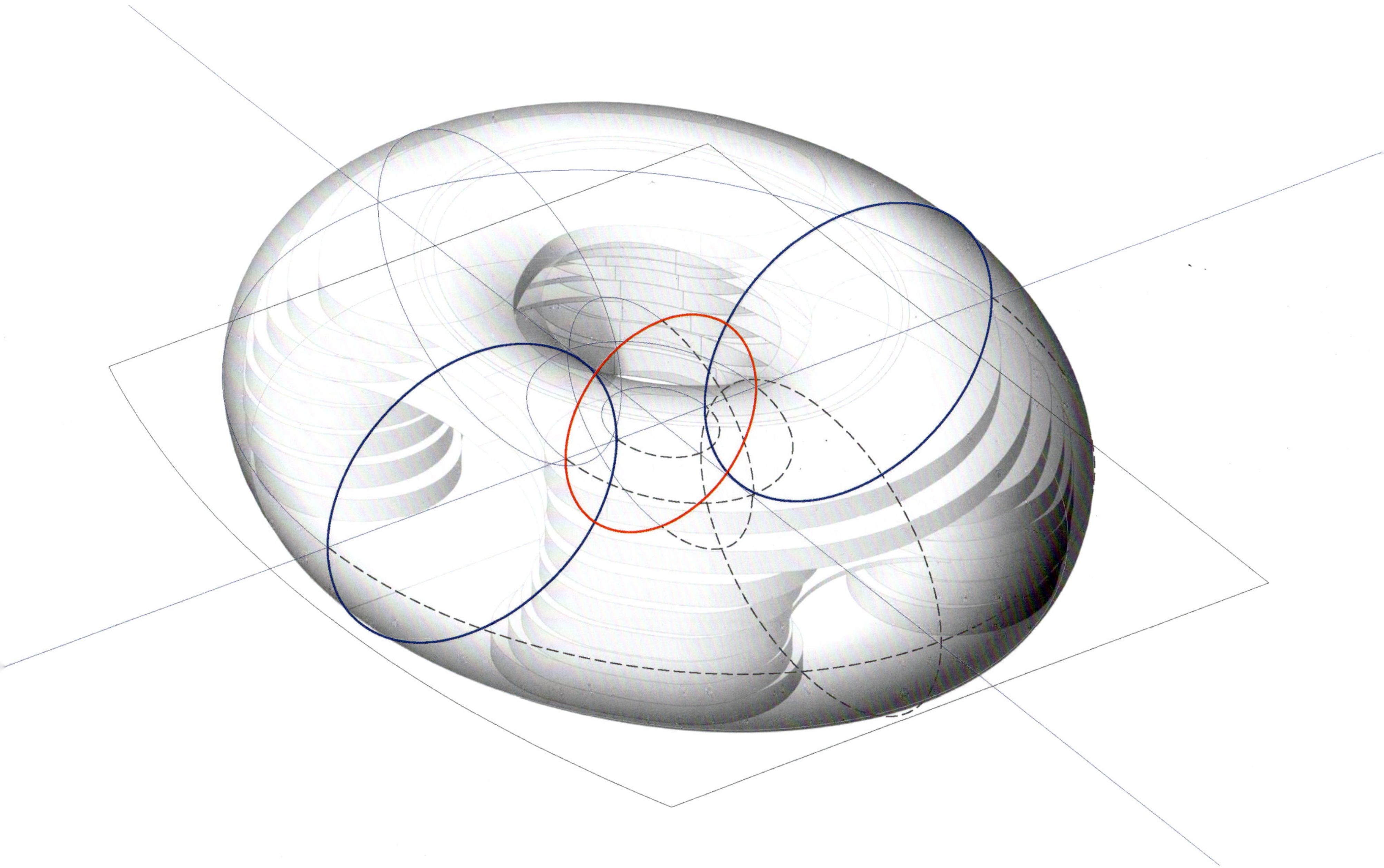

Three-dimensional study for
Jewel Changi Airport

TERRACE ARC RADII AND CENTER POINT TABLE

ARC	RADIUS	CENTER POINT
ARC A		N 43783, E -43898
ARC B	33000	N 40717, E -38177
ARC C	31000	N 40947, E -36379
ARC D	29000	N 41260, E -34620
ARC E	27000	N 41587 E -31219
ARC F	25000	N 41931, E -31219
ARC G	23000	N 42688, E -29484
ARC H	21000	N 43275, E -27820
ARC I	19000	N 43764, E -26188
ARC J	17000	N 44084, E -24578
ARC K	16000	N 44877, E -23958
ARC L	15000	N 43423, E - 23360
ARC M	14000	N 45831, E - 22769
ARC N	13000	N 46121, E -22178
ARC O	12000	N 46357, E -21586
ARC P	11000	N 46591, E -20994
ARC Q	10000	N 46654, E -20395
ARC R	9000	N 46591, E -19792
ARC S	8500	N 46612, E -19693

NOTE: CENTER POINTS MIRRORED ABOUT CL. 1 FOR EAST QUADRANT

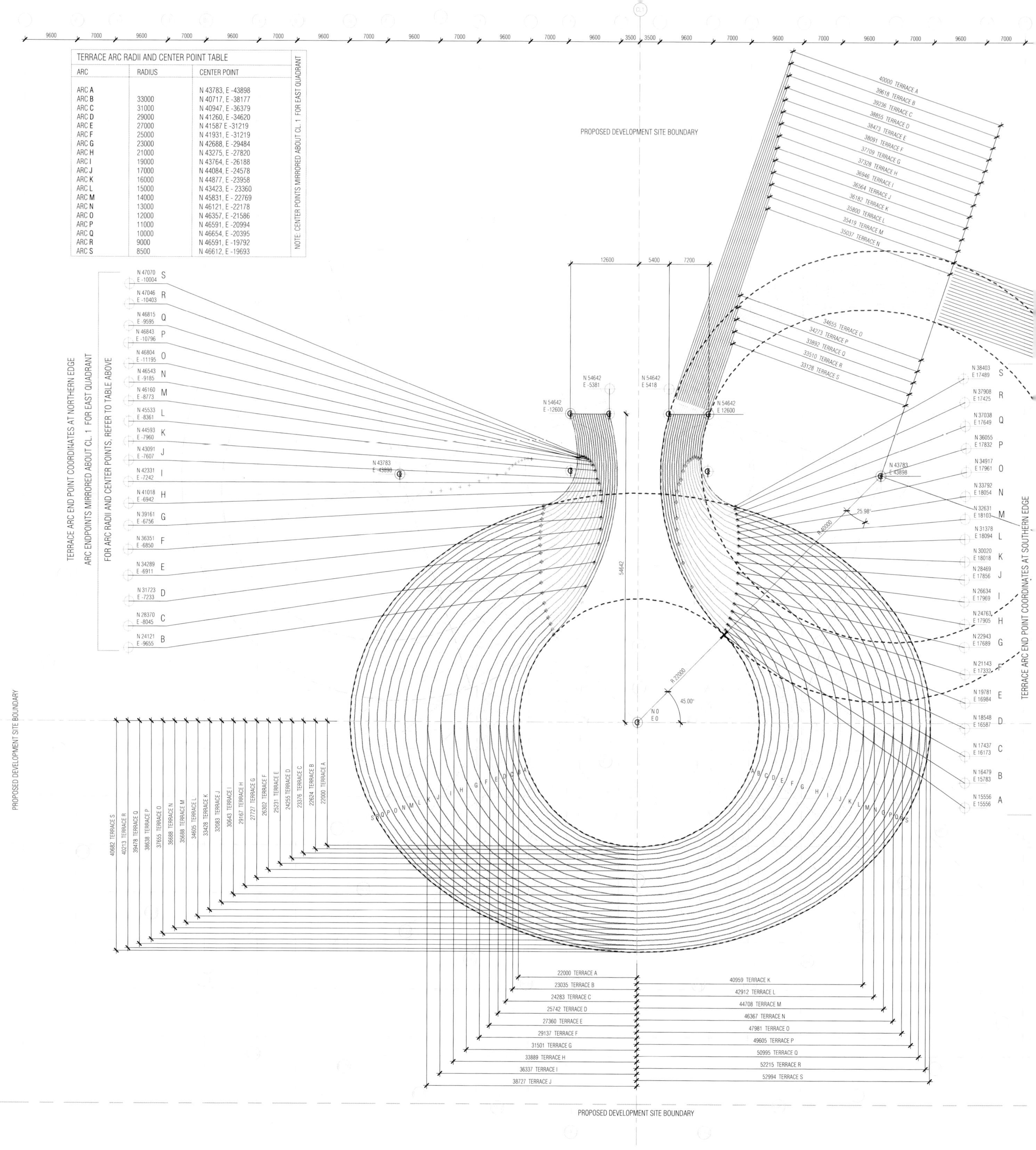

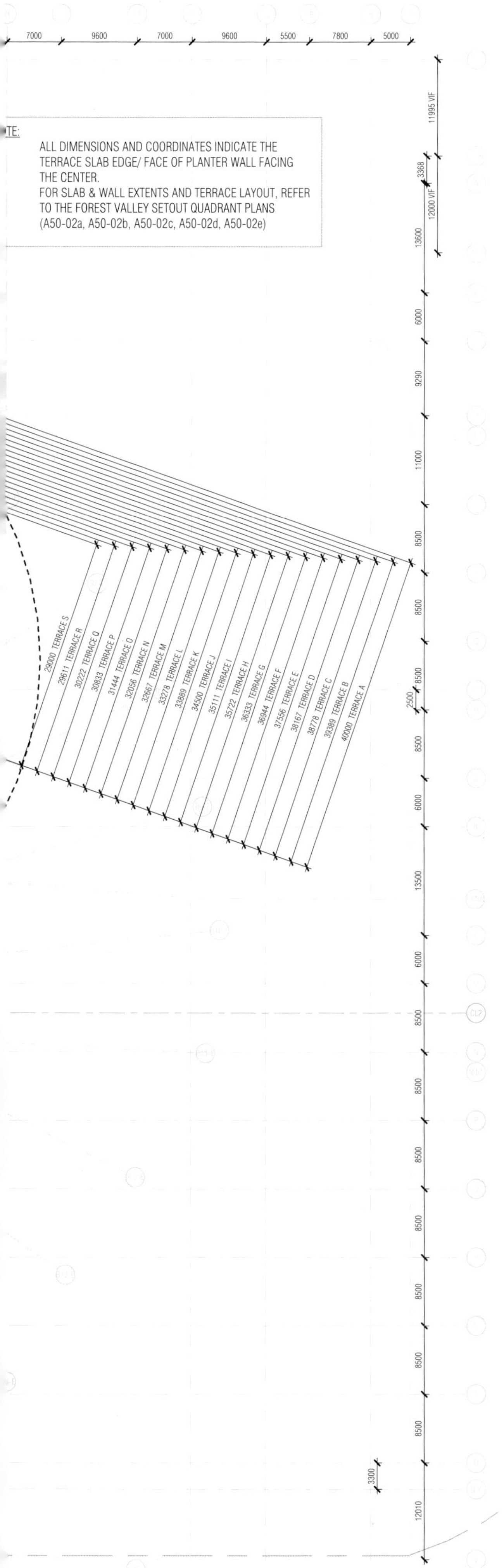

of the entire team to develop a solution: automated door systems at each entry that would act as air locks, the first of their kind.

Too often, a building falls short of matching the illustrations that depict its concept design. Today, one of the greatest compliments we receive is when people look at a photo of the building and cannot decipher whether it is real or a fantasy. The essays to follow show how the assembled team was able to come together in a symphony of collaboration to choreograph Singapore's next great public attraction.

Parametric drawing illustrates the complex geometries of the Forest Valley garden

Above: Light filters through the Rain Vortex's crown as workers perch on temporary construction scaffolding below

Left: The Forest Valley terraces immediately before tree planting begins

A Landscape of Wonder

PWP Landscape Architecture

Adam Greenspan
Lead Landscape Architect

When Safdie Architects first approached us about joining them to develop Jewel Changi Airport, I wondered why on earth we would be making an indoor garden in Singapore—one of the world's best environments for plant growth. But it occurred to me, as I thought about Singapore's hot, humid climate, that a great indoor park could have the potential for all-day use. It could introduce people, in a comfortably air-conditioned airport, to the wonders of plant life, and open their eyes to the natural world. Jewel could have the potential to be more than a building and more than a garden: an integrated landscape where people would work, shop, relax, play, and reflect on living systems in the contemporary world.

A good idea always comes with an interesting challenge. Most indoor gardens are developed as plant displays and presented in conservatories specifically designed for plant needs, not human ones. In fact, their interior climates often resemble the muggy outdoor climate of Singapore. But at Jewel, plants would not be the primary users of the building, people would. I wondered how we could work to bridge these competing needs, assuring the health of the plants and meeting the requirements of future visitors.

"Moshe, are you willing to treat the interiors very differently from your other buildings, for the sake of plants?" I asked during our initial conversation at breakfast on the 57th-floor SkyPark at Marina Bay Sands. "Of course!" Moshe responded, "What do you want? We will do what needs to be done. The garden is central to this place!"

With Moshe's certainty, I began to imagine—and to remember—grand and dramatic landscapes that would captivate and envelop visitors. Misty forest trails, both magical and inspiring. Enormous terraced agricultural valleys that I have visited across the world, from Asia to South America, to Napa Valley. Great waterfalls that change the climate and the experience of the world around them. Special moments in the forest during and after a rain. Summer afternoons in San Francisco when the fog rolls in as fast as cars move across the Golden Gate Bridge. I also thought of the amazing Rain Tree allée along East Coast Parkway, carrying you from Changi Airport itself to Central Singapore: its audacious scale and power, and the great spreads of its trees, their trunks thick with aerial vegetation.

Back at our office in California, we decided that this place, the interior of Jewel, should be more than a garden. Neither a decorative display nor a simple botanical exhibit within a building, but rather a landscape of grandeur and wonder. A landscape that would reveal its own organic order, surprise people, and wrap in them a sense of wonder, and most importantly, a sense of place. We wanted to create a constructed landscape that would be like nowhere else in the world. At

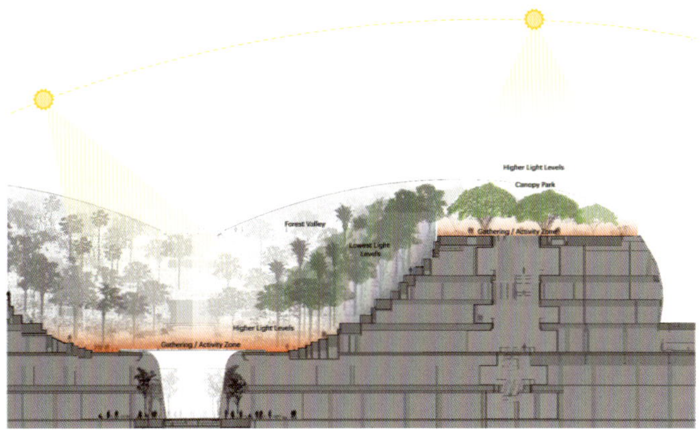

Shade-providing trees and flowering plants were used in zones of high light levels to create a comfortable and interesting experience. Human activity is concentrated around the Rain Vortex, lower garden terraces, and Canopy Park, in the shade of the trees.

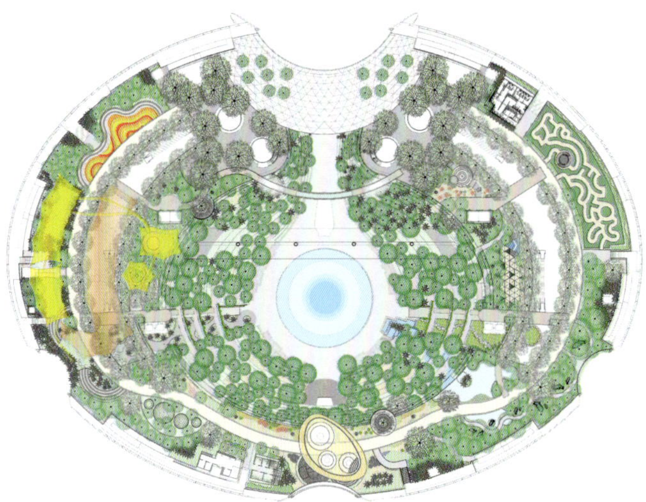

Overall landscape plan of Canopy Park and the Forest Valley

the same time, we wanted Jewel to become one of Singapore's well-known destinations, such as Gardens by the Bay, Marina Bay Sands, the Singapore Botanic Gardens, and, of course, Changi Airport. All would work together to form Singapore's image and identity.

Landscape Spaces

In conceiving this interior world, we decided that its landscape should feel true to nature—as if it somehow grew inside the building. The plant palette, and even the hardscape materials, should be derived from nature and sustain themselves over the years. We began conceiving two connected landscapes that would respond to the designed site, while in turn creating different conditions for their users.

The first of these landscapes, the Forest Valley, would be a unified forest of closely planted, tall-trunked, vertical trees, allowing a great deal of air and light to pass beneath their canopies. These trees would dance down garden terraces at irregular spacing, similar to shading trees employed by farmers in tea and coffee plantations.

Together with Safdie Architects we refined a bowl shape, where floor levels would be divided into multiple terraced planter levels that would get wider as they approached the Forest Valley floor. The lower garden terraces, occupied by visitors, would integrate stone paving. Small garden patios would be carved out for people to spend time quietly or focus on the Rain Vortex, with its light and water show high above. As the terraces ascended, they would get thinner and taller. Two walking trails would climb the valley all the way up to Level 5, allowing access to the mall at every floor along the hike. We also developed a cascading waterfall that we called Cataract Falls within the terraces of the valley, its source starting as a pool within the park above. The source pool would overflow and create sheeted falls down the terraces to the forest floor.

The woodland understory planting in the Forest Valley would change related to the elevation of the planter terraces and corresponding to the varied light levels available below the tree canopy. We found that the lowest and highest planting zones would receive more light at soil level than the mid elevations because the forest trees would shade the mid-levels more intensely.

On Level 5, high above the valley we imagined what we called the "Horizon Garden," offering views to the horizon across the airport. Now known as Canopy Park, it would include more floor area than all of the levels in the Forest Valley combined. Located at the highest elevation of the building, closest to the glass enclosure, it would receive the highest light levels, allowing for a range of horticultural attractions. While bright light is important for the growth and health of plants, direct sun can reduce comfort levels for people. To ensure the best environment for both visitors and plants, we proposed that along with the glass façade and the air-conditioning system, the planting design would be part of an integrated environmental comfort infrastructure. To that end, we proposed a continuous, shade-providing tree canopy for Canopy Park, harkening back to the Rain Trees whose canopies extend over East Coast Parkway.

Canopy Park was conceived as a place where visitors could experience a variety of attractions. We worked toward a palette of nearly all natural materials, and an ensemble of attractions that focused on re-creating experiences in nature. Underneath a continuous shading canopy of trees we would carve out spaces for special experiences, including: the Canopy Bridge, Foggy Bowls, Climbing and Bouncing Nets, Mirror and Hedge Mazes, Sculptural Discovery Slide, Topiary Jungle Walk, Water Garden, and Chromatic Flower Garden, as well as a large event plaza.

Gardens

In addition to the major landscape spaces within Jewel, there would be a series of discreet gardens performing specific tasks and offering special experiences, helping this constructed organism function as a whole. The first garden type, Canyons, would be two crevasse-like gardens cutting through all levels of the Forest Valley. Early on we programmed these canyon gardens as the locations for vertical access within the landscape. Glass elevators would travel through Palm Canyon to the west and Bamboo Canyon to the east. Trails that ran up the Forest Valley would cross the canyons repeatedly as they switched back to climb in elevation. Vertical palms and bamboo plants could eventually reach three-to-four stories tall, knitting together the experience and threading between the bridges that cross the canyon at every level.

The Gateway Gardens were conceived as four-story-tall vertical scoops cut out of the retail levels directly behind the building's glass façade. These gardens would face outward to the public and the greater airport landscape. Each Gateway Garden would contain more vertical space than floor area, acting as billboards or living façades, and broadcasting to the world some of the surprise and wonder that exists inside Jewel.

To achieve these hanging gardens, we worked closely with the architects and structural engineers to coordinate concepts that could be elevated and hung three stories in the air. The Hanging Fern Garden in the East Gateway would feature 4-meter-tall columns of fern compositions that reference the epiphytic ferns growing on the trunks of trees in Singapore. The West Gateway Garden would feature giant hanging orbs made of Tillandsia air plants and Bromeliads with flowers that also grow on local trees. The South Gateway Garden, which faces the control tower and Airport Boulevard, would employ palms of two distinct forms and heights to create a green elevation when looking from the outside, and frame views of the control tower and the airport for visitors looking from inside Jewel.

A Truly Integrated Design

While the first thing anyone would notice about Jewel's 2,400 square meter landscape is that it is indoors, it may not register that it is also built entirely on structure. In choosing Jewel's plant palette and creating a space of splendor, comfort, safety, and well-being in such a complex, the constructed space called for deep collaboration with architects, environmental engineers, structural engineers, and many others.

Airport management had determined, for instance, that Jewel should measure 24°C year-round in its visitor-occupied areas. But we quickly discovered that few plants live in such an environment, and those that do are not commonly found commercially. As we refined the design with our highly technical team, we honed our plant palette goals, basing our recommendations on resilient and sturdy species that could perform well in a conservatory setting.

Moving ahead, we further detailed the species and plant palette based on countless more variables (humidity, growth rates, and so on), and the professional expertise of partners such as ICN Design, our local landscape architect, which has a long history of working on some of the largest and most complex landscape installations in Singapore. We also enlisted a global team of consultants, and connected with horticulturalists from Gardens by the Bay, Kew Gardens, the San Francisco Conservatory of Flowers, an interior plant importer in the Netherlands, and zoo directors and curators in Zürich. Additionally, we met with grow light manufacturers in the San Francisco Bay Area and living reef specialists who have developed lights for the sustenance and display of coral.

We performed our own research—with the help of facilities worldwide—related to the specific growth and requirements of particular species indoors. Finding little data on the growth of ornamental plants in conservatory settings, or under artificial light, we reviewed conservatory species at places ranging from the National United States Botanical Garden in Washington, D.C. and Gardens by the Bay in Singapore to Palm House at KewGardens and the terminal gardens at Changi Airport. As a result, we specified trees that had a track record of performing well in a variety of climatic conditions.

Tree installation at Canopy Park. Trees were hoisted to Level 5 via a 100-ton crane, loaded onto a wheeled platform, and maneuvered into place using a forklift and vast amounts of manpower.

Continued research included advanced dynamic modeling through which we estimated the stratification of temperatures and humidity within the building, including the effect Rain Vortex could have on the space. Based on this data we expected Jewel's climate to support a range of plant species somewhere between a tropical, tropical montane, and subtropical palette. Our team also developed a sophisticated testing plan, which included construction of a temporary coolhouse called the "polytunnel" that could be set to the same light, humidity, and temperature conditions as Jewel. We aimed for the contractor to use this facility to test additional shrub and groundcover species so we could assess which previously untested plants would be able to acclimate to Jewel's climate.

After we made our final plant and tree selections, landscape contractor TEHC International expertly located sources from all over the world, with the majority coming from the Southeast Asia/ Australia region. As a team we scheduled a series of plant-hunting safaris where representatives from PWP, ICN, TEHC and Jewel went out with local tree growers to find and tag the material needed for the project. More than 3,000 trees and palms were initially tagged for Jewel, with about 2,500 finally used in the project, plus 10 percent surplus material brought into Singapore to be used as replacements, if necessary. Ultimately, trees and palms were tagged in 12 countries and shipped to Singapore over land and by sea.

Mock-ups and Installation

One of the most exciting parts of the early construction process was the creation of full-scale mock-ups of the main landscape elements, including paving designs, Canopy Park attractions, plant combinations, hanging garden constructions, and, most impressively, a complete portion of the Forest Valley terrace garden system. Through this Forest Valley visual mock-up we were able to better understand the overall impression of the elements, and to test and understand the systems required to function within the final design, such as drainage, soil space and volume, paving, and lighting. The visual mock-up that was constructed as part of Jewel was the largest and most helpful mock-up that we have ever been part of during the design process. With it, the contractor was also able to assess the overall construction strategy, including methods and processes for installation.

After the mock-ups, dynamic modeling, design work, and plant selection, our team's final effort took place in Singapore in close coordination with ICN, the landscape architect, and TEHC, the landscape contractor. As the pre-grow nursery we had constructed filled up, the project's vastness became clear, and it was apparent that we had indeed brought a new forest to Singapore. As we watched Jewel being built, it was hard to believe that the acres of plants and trees could fit inside. But even these trees, some of the largest we have ever been able to get for a project, appeared small inside the mega structure, which we joked had the power to devour them.

The PWP team engaged in repeated evening conference calls and nightly instant messaging, as well as monthly to bi-weekly site visits to review and adjust the installation to account for, for instance, the fact that tree sizes and shapes cannot be standardized. We also worked to optimize design goals at every location, maximizing the wonder and thrill that visitors could experience on the climbing nets or walking across the fog bridge by pairing unexpected plant material of dramatic scale where its impact could be appreciated. Finally, all the plants arrived. The systems were tested and retested, modified, and choreographed to be sure that visitors would get an incredible experience. Meanwhile, Changi's newest botanical residents in Jewel could finally stretch their roots and their shoots and settle into their new home for the long haul.

Through collaboration and coordination between expert design professionals across disciplines, Jewel has been realized as the most integrated experience of hybrid landscape and architecture that we have ever been part of. Walking into the Forest Valley, with the forest around you, sun pouring in from above, and rain falling from the sky, is like experiencing a natural wonder, not an interior garden, or any garden that I know. When taken as a whole—the gardens, retail, event plazas, attractions, train, and arterial connections—Jewel is truly a landscape that has a life of its own.

The carefully collaborative work here, and the evolving ecosystems that it has set in motion, reminds us all of the significance of landscape on the built environment. Jewel is a testament to teamwork, and a team's vision for designing and constructing a place that can sustain life. As we look to all cities and all places of "nature" in our world, we are now coming to realize that they are all landscapes that require conscious effort to change, adapt, maintain, and manage as they grow. I hope that what we have created together at Jewel can be a showcase of the potential for a landscape of the future.

CANOPY BRIDGE

Engineering an Icon

BuroHappold

Craig Schwitter
Cristobal Correa
Lead Engineers,
Roof Structure & Façades

When was the last time you walked through an airport, a theater, or an office atrium and looked up? Normally we look around us—sometimes pleased, sometimes disappointed in the spaces—but rarely affected. When the many elements of a public space come together to create a memorable, inspiring, affecting *experience*, that's when we have moved beyond mere engineering or architecture.

Great public spaces are also a result of intense collaboration, where all team members are integral to the design, and all the finished parts are synchronized, effortlessly. Great teams challenge us to push the boundaries of our technical skills to the next level. Jewel is such a project. A partnership story between engineering and architecture, and something that in the end is much more than just a roof.

The Idea

It all started in 2012 with a competition-winning design wedged between existing terminals at Changi Airport. Safdie Architects' first images of Jewel showed an awe-inspiring roof that spanned large distances, but was also transparent and permeable. A weightless expanse that floated above one of the world's largest indoor gardens and turned down at its center to create the world's largest indoor waterfall. It was daring, and our team was hooked on how to help create it.

The form and geometry of this roof would end up occupying us for many months, and then years. There were conflicting and sometimes competing needs. It needed to be light, while at the same time strong enough to span great distances. It needed to appear as a single unbroken form, while at the same time performing multiple structural tasks as it spanned from the perimeter of the building to the waterfall. And above all it needed to take a complex, three-dimensional form and break it down into easily understood, easily connected components that would appear unbroken and elegant. The viewer had to *feel* beauty before having any understanding of how it was standing up.

First It Has to Stand...

The space allocated for Jewel was at a crossroads between terminals, connecting to an entrance concourse and traversed by an existing airport train. Safdie Architects' idea of creating a vast central valley here, with a waterfall at its center, meant extremely large spans.

The need to ensure enough structural strength to manage such ambitious spans without support columns, led to the creation of a toroidal (like a donut or bagel) roof composed of a single-layer steel-and-glass system. Most glass roof systems are compression driven,

steel diagrid installation

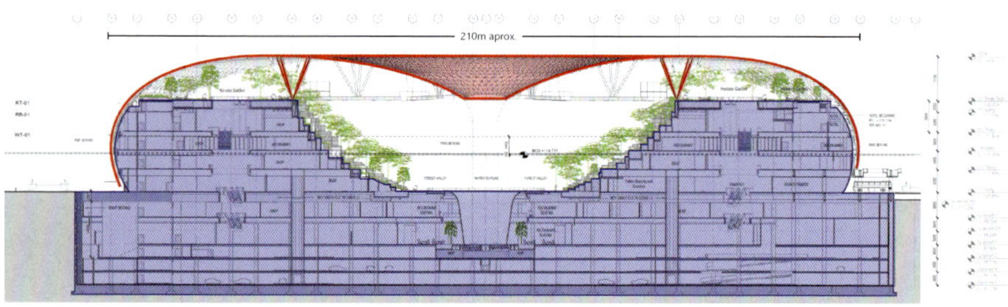

Building section illustrating division of base building and roof structure, as well as the 210 meter span of the glass and steel diagrid roof

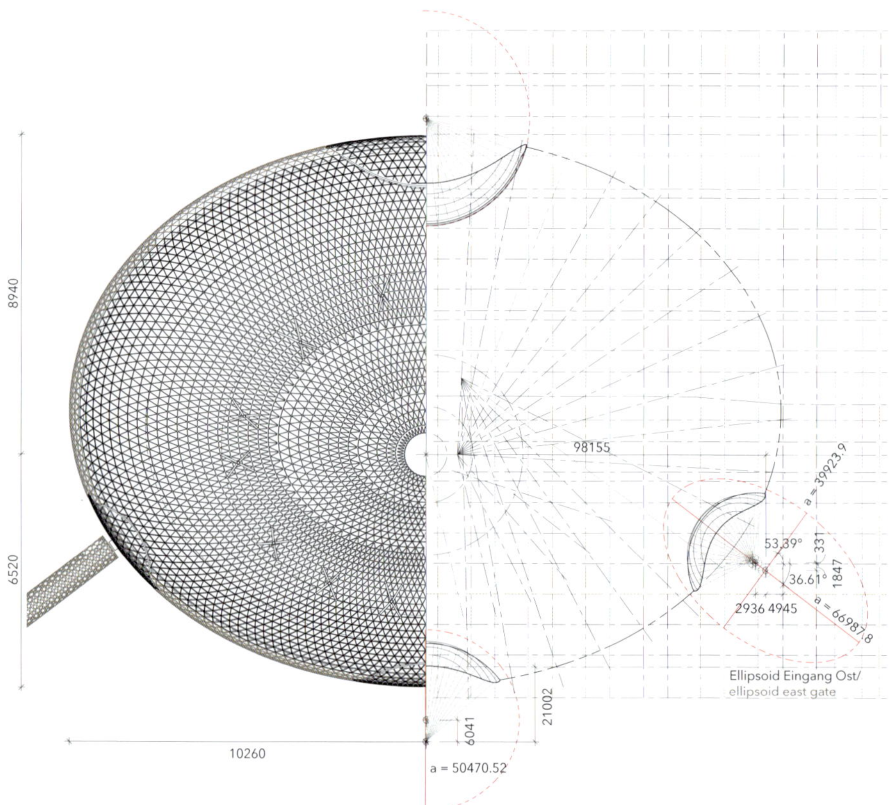

Structural roof plan

meaning their shell structures contain only modest bending forces. The shape of Jewel is different. It is not symmetrical about its long axis, and it uses internal supports. It was obvious that this shape would contain much greater stress variation than any structure we had designed before.

So how do the forces flow? It is helpful to see the Jewel roof in a series of sections. The inner section is a tension cone, with all elements essentially suspended and pulling down at the structural center. These membrane tensions flow in both the hoop and the meridional direction of the structure. Steel is efficient in taking tension forces, so we expected the members in this area of the shell to be the most delicate.

Next is the outer section. This section is mostly in compression, again with membrane forces in both the hoop and meridional direction. There is good arch action here, so we expected reasonably sized steel members.

Finally, there are the middle supports. This is where the tension and compression fields meet and it gets interesting. First, the structure needs to *contain* the tensions created in the suspended middle section. It does this by creating a tangential "compression ring," which is part of the shell itself. Like the rim of a bicycle wheel, the highest portion of the shell acts as a horizontal truss—effectively holding the tensions of the suspended center in place.

But other forces are generated here, particularly bending out of the plane of the shell. A simple analogy of a diving board demonstrates how bending forces—very large in places—are created. These bending forces would increase the shell depth in these areas, and create visible manifestations of what was going on. This appealed to the design team, as it showed a specific reaction to the forces in the roof and a visual response to the forces.

Key to this structural scheme was understanding that with advanced fabrication technology we would be able to vary our steel sizes as we moved through the roof. This would allow us to keep our idea of a single-layer grid shell, allowing light, air, and openness. The structure's thinness is crucial, acting as a membrane between the interior and exterior, and modulating air, sunlight, and water, all essential in creating comfort.

To further give a sensation of clarity and elegance to the structure, the width of all steel pieces was kept constant, with only the depth and wall thickness of the steel allowed to vary to accommodate areas with increased load—particularly at the support columns, where bending is introduced into the shell.

As we developed these designs, we realized that although we were creating individual steel elements and glass triangles, we were also creating families of components that might possibly be grouped together for fabrication, depending on the tolerances that might be possible to achieve in fabrication and detail.

A Question of Geometry

But there was still the question of how to achieve the transparency of this form. The analogy might be that we understood the shape we wanted, but we did not yet know what it would be made of.

The curved roof form had to be discretized, or broken down into smaller components. The easiest way to do this with flat pieces of glass is by using triangles and creating a "diagrid" of steel pieces to support the glass panels. Horizontal lines or hoops were created on the surface to create a feeling of continuity with the horizontal floor plates of the building. These would be overlaid by continuous bias or vertical elements—or both—to break the form down into triangles and create a swooshing, dynamic form that we all liked. We looked at many patterns to find one that would be most pleasing to the eye.

But how large or small should these triangles be? The larger these triangles became, the larger the steel element would need to become, and the more faceted the form would appear. How would the size of these elements feel to someone in the space, and what sort of transparency would it provide? The best way to understand this was by traveling to see other forms that had been triangulated and examining how scale was impacted by the overall size of the project as well as the distance from the person in the building. A larger triangle might not create the most transparent roof!

Another limitation on size came from manufacturing and construction concerns. It was important to keep the triangles to a size that would allow them to be manufactured by many suppliers. This would allow open, competitive bidding, and ensure the best price for the client.

As the discretization progressed, another design issue appeared. As the continuous diagonal lines advanced from the perimeter of our roof to the center, the triangles become progressively smaller, congesting elements, hurting transparency, and increasing the difficulty to execute. This necessitated a process of pruning—cutting back some bias lines in order to maintain the scale of triangular elements. This had to be done in a way that would appear natural, by not breaking the flow of the surface while also allowing for the smooth transfer of structural forces through the shell.

How Would We Build It?

Without huge advancements in shell technology, Jewel would not exist. Historically, shells have been constructed as domes made out of masonry materials—only good in compression, not tension. In the early 20th century, the advancement of reinforced concrete shell design moved to ever thinner and bolder shapes. By the end of that century, glass-and-steel shells, cheaper and more transparent, had supplanted concrete, creating large spaces with high levels of daylight. And as automated fabrication became more prevalent near the turn of the millennium, steel grid shells were born. Now single-layer systems of steel, with a great variety of geometry and transparency, could be engineered, fabricated, and built.

Jewel Changi Airport's grid shell roof is made up of approximately 5,000 nodes, 14,000 steel elements, and 10,000 triangular glass panels, all different. But while unique, every piece of hardware shared a consistent set of geometrical rules and a systemized construction and connection strategy.

During manufacture each was identified and tracked with an individual code that made it possible to identify its location in the overall grid shell building information model (BIM) computer file. This organization was essential: putting together Jewel was similar to assembling a massive puzzle, where each piece only fits in one precise location.

Demonstrating the simplification of complexity that has come about with modern manufacturing processes, each of the thousands of components was produced using advanced, and often automated methods.

The steel box sections were manufactured from straight steel plates by Singapore-based Yongnam, which used robots to precisely cut and weld the pieces together. The nodes were manufactured by MERO in Germany, which used a 3D computer numerical control (CNC) milling machine to create nodes that were stubbed at precise angles to meet the connecting steel elements. The pieces were then painted and drilled with bolt holes where necessary. (About 20 percent of the node-to-steel-piece connections were welded.) The glass triangles were manufactured and assembled at facilities in China specializing in glass fabrication, lamination, and assembly. They were cut from industry-standard rectangular sheets that fit into lamination ovens.

A very large visual mock-up was created during design to ensure that all components—glass, steel, nodes, geometry, and the like—would work well together, and to allow for fine tuning of the

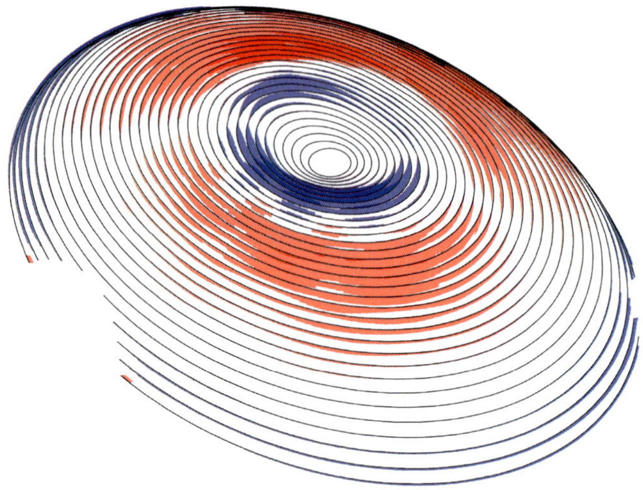

Analysis diagram studying the axial forces in the roof's structural hoops

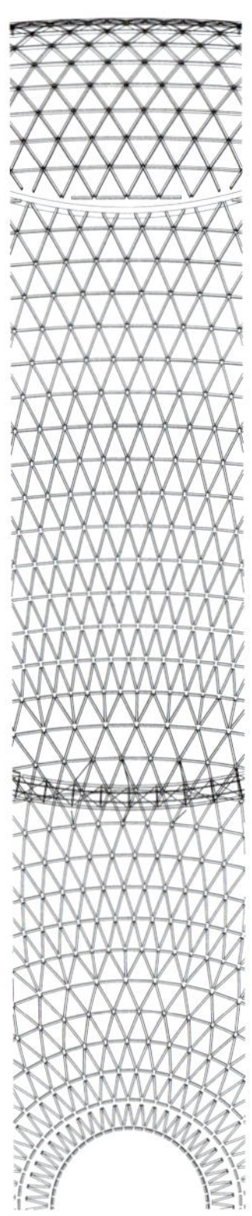

Enlarged structural plan shows the roof geometry "discretization," in which the overall form was broken down into consistently scaled panels no larger than 2.5 meters in length

final design. This was especially significant for the project team to understand the level of workmanship that was required to execute the enclosure design. Performance mock-ups were also created to verify the level of waterproofing of the design. This was done in areas of critical detailing by applying negative pressure on the inside of the mock-up test chamber, and by spraying water on the exterior.

Engineering an Iconic Space

Jewel is a technical marvel. From digital engineering analysis to automated fabrication, and from precision manufacturing to on-site assembly, the structure represents radical advancements in emerging techniques that are still new in the hands of architects, fabricators, and constructors. Like most exquisite engineering, it makes seemingly impossible feats seem effortless and invisible. Its structure sets a new benchmark in grid shell design, pushing the boundaries of form and structure in terms of single layer systems and the use of steel in shells. Its geometrical form and thousands of non-repeatable panels requires deep fabrication and construction intelligence to assemble and construct.

Jewel also represents a new type of enclosure, combining structure, façade, and environment. It brings the outside environment inside its single-layer grid shell, allowing and modulating generous gifts of light, air, and openness. The roof structure is less a traditional shelter and more a membrane or environmental filter. The structural design addresses this in being robust in performance, but thin in profile.

What is an experience, if not one that a visitor will feel through daylight streaming into the interior, thermal comfort created by the waterfall, or an acoustic sense of peace within the massive gardens? What makes a space great is the invisible hand of a designer that shapes and creates these conditions. Jewel recognizes the grid shell roof—freed from traditional geometric and structural constraints—as the *key* component to creating this experience.

Jewel also represents the great effort of a large group of people—architects, engineers, builders. It has a visionary client that understands the future of aviation and the airport experience. A great building is about relationships in the end, a collective and collaboration effort, not a singular vision or voice. These many voices have created a public space like no other in the world, and an experience that has surpassed any airport. The bar is set high, and Jewel will serve and delight the weary traveler, the casual visitor, and ultimately the citizens of Singapore for years to come.

Steel roof diagrid installation as viewed from one of several tower cranes

Glazing installation in progress

Creating a 21st-Century Glasshouse

Atelier Ten

Patrick Bellew
Meredith Davey
Henry Woon
Environmental Designers

Green Singapore

In 1967, Prime Minister Lee Kuan Yew presented his vision of Singapore as a "City in a Garden," a goal that has driven its physical identity ever since. Singapore's tree-lined boulevards, large parks, sky gardens, green connectors, and many other landscape devices now define a place where there is an almost continuous physical connection between man and the natural world.

In addition to providing Singapore a clear identity as one of the world's greenest places, the green cover that makes up some 47 percent of its area limits much of its equatorial sunshine and reduces its temperature. It also absorbs pollutants, filters particulates, and provides oxygen.

With this profound impact in mind—along with the enthusiastic support of Moshe Safdie, who clearly had something pathbreaking in mind—it seemed completely appropriate that Jewel Changi Airport, the new gateway to Singapore, should represent the very best, and greenest, that the country has to offer.

A New Kind of Glasshouse

The history of conditioned planting under glass consists mainly of buildings that consume very large amounts of energy. Glass is generally not a great insulator, and the greenhouse effect is an immutable reality. Victorian-era glasshouses, such as those at Kew Gardens and the New York Botanical Garden, were single-glazed with cast glass to maximize light and solar gain, requiring huge amounts of resources to heat and cool. Modernist versions, like the Climatron in St. Louis, introduced conditioning innovations like "swirling" air flow systems, which made conditions more comfortable, but still couldn't completely solve the energy conundrum. Recent advances have had more success, like the U.K.'s Eden Project, a bubble-like structure in Cornwall, England, that balances performance and sustainability through advanced building management systems, an insulating, double-layered ETFE skin, sustainably sourced materials, and a renewable energy program using rooftop photovoltaics and water harvesting.

At Jewel Changi Airport, our team needed to perform an especially challenging balancing act: introducing natural light, showcasing nature, and providing constant thermal human comfort in terms of temperature, humidity, and air movement, all while minimizing the building's energy demands. We undertook a considerable amount of research to get this balance right, while ensuring that the systems in the space would be as concealed as possible so visitors would not be aware of the technology and equipment keeping them comfortable.

Construction of the Level 1 floor slab includes integrated chilled flooring. The Forest Valley planters above have integrated displacement cooling systems

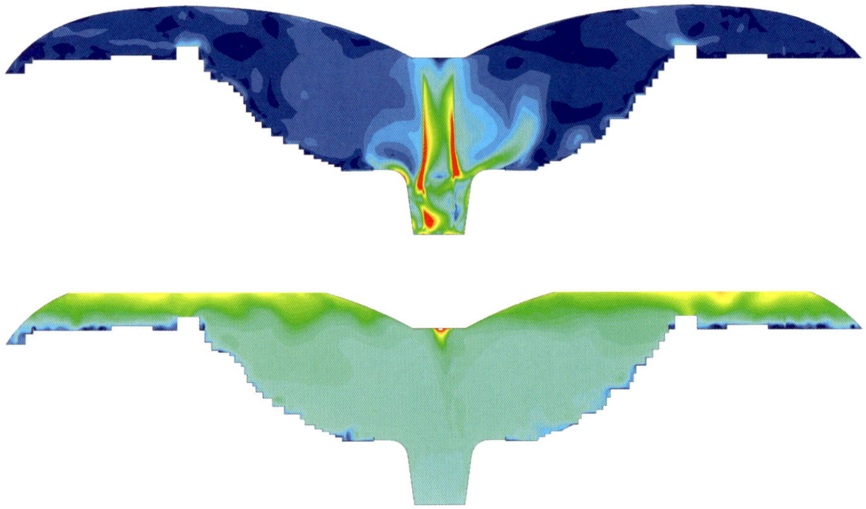

Modeling air speeds (top) and temperatures (bottom) to inform the design before commencing construction

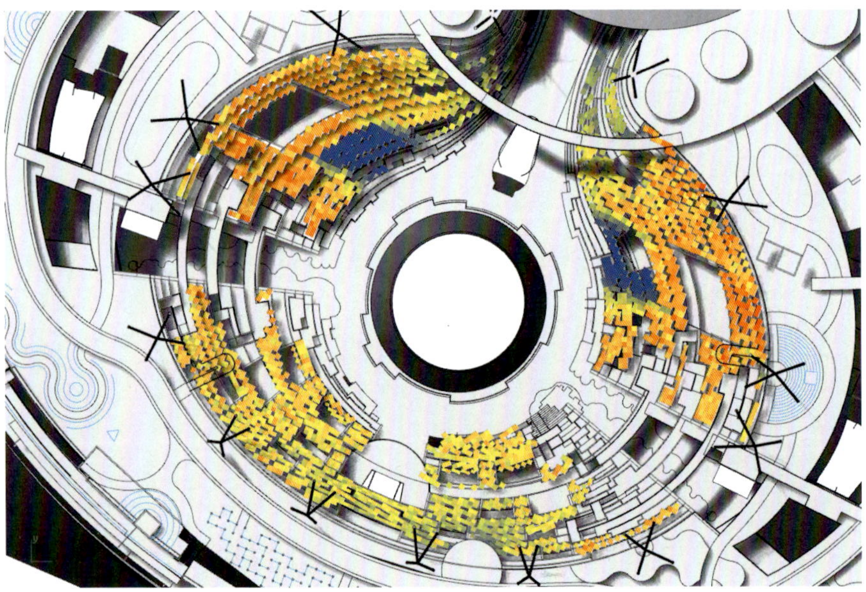

Mapping daylight levels and solar exposure for the Forest Valley. Generating these maps allowed the landscape team to determine appropriate daylight levels for each garden's plantings.

Modeling Daylight

Resolving the competing demands between heat and light was the basis for many months of discussion between the design team and client. The main issue was that plants typically need higher light levels than people, which introduces elevated levels of unpredictable solar heat. Our façade optimization therefore sought to ensure that light levels would vary in different parts of the building based on planting locations and palette, while still minimizing the loads on conditioning systems.

Using a combination of bespoke ray tracing and illuminance prediction software linked to the architect's 3D BIM model, we modeled the light coming through each triangular cell of the grid shell roof for each hour of the year. This modeling technique facilitated greater design and engineering flexibility, and allowed us to evaluate many different glazing materials and surface coatings in terms of energy demand and use.

The glass coating that was eventually selected for Jewel admits 62 percent of the sun's energy as visible light, while allowing only 33 percent of that energy as heat. A frit pattern, which creates the building's varied external appearance, was applied in different densities to reflect broadband radiation in areas where light is less critical. Where daylight is not required for plant growth, such as the event plaza, fritting and motorized shading devices further reduce air-conditioning requirements.

Apart from comfort implications, the ability to limit solar heat gain while still delivering high daylight levels was vital to reducing the air-conditioning requirement in the indoor garden, which in turn would reduce servicing needs, plantroom space, and energy use.

Our collaboration with PWP Landscape Architecture was particularly important to this process. As the daylight analysis produced an understanding of the available light in particular areas, we took an iterative process to asses appropriate plant selections and landscape responses. Conversely species that required higher light levels were accommodated by adjusting the surface properties of the glass to shine more light into these areas.

Thermal Comfort and Systems

While plants are mainly affected by the overall energy they receive from the sun, humans are more concerned with instantaneous conditions, aka comfort. To maintain well-being while minimizing energy demand, our intent was to only condition areas that people would inhabit, and to work with the architectural forms of the space to optimize the semi-natural air flows from features like the Rain Vortex.

In the tropics, manually operated punkah fans are still widely used in non-conditioned spaces, while in most conditioned spaces it is normal to limit air movement because of concerns with cold air and drafts. We developed something of a hybrid in Jewel, creating regular zones of higher-than-normal air movement, which give the impression of a semi-outdoor environment and provide additional cooling effects to offset exposure to solar gain.

Jewel's air movement is mainly achieved by supplying cool, dry air into the space at low levels, but at a comparatively high velocity, producing an effect akin to a light breeze. In addition, the majority of the hard floor surfaces have chilled water piped through them. The conditioning system relies on heat from the space stratifying and rising to higher levels (plants are more forgiving of heat than humans), confining the cooling to the occupied zone.

A series of lab experiments, using a radiant heat source to replicate the effects of solar gain, were conducted to confirm what would constitute acceptable air velocities inside the space. The tests were calibrated by taking thermal readings of visitors inside the flower dome at Gardens by the Bay, then recreating those results inside the lab.

The Rain Vortex waterfall at the center of the building provides a minor cooling effect on the space through direct evaporation. But its disruptive air movement proved to be a complex challenge for our hybrid displacement air system. Our computational fluid dynamics tests showed that its falling water droplets would pull stratified hot air from the top of the space down to the lower levels, creating extra heat and humidity around its base. Subsequent modeling showed that a continuous glass balustrade around the base (which was installed) would serve to redirect the air vertically and prevent the disruption to the air in the surrounding areas.

Skytrain Tunnels

One of the most striking features of Jewel is the Skytrain that travels through the building, over the Forest Valley. In the original design the train's track was enclosed in a glass tube, intended to prevent cool air from leaking outside. However, the glass tube obstructed views of the garden and vortex and there was a strong push to eliminate it.

After extensive analysis the team opted to incorporate four sets of interlocked fast action doors—similar to those used for vehicle access to cold stores in warehouses—into the tunnels approaching the entry and exit to Jewel. These operate sequentially and rapidly to minimize air leakage. The Skytrain slows on entry to minimize the piston effect of air being pushed in front of the train and dragged out behind it.

Jewel is located at a point where trains arriving from other terminals cross over, meaning they tend to arrive from each side simultaneously. Each train pushes a small amount of air into the building, but at relatively low velocity. This warm air is then sucked back out by the train going in the opposite direction out of the building. Extensive computational fluid dynamics (CFD) simulations demonstrated the effectiveness of this proposal, helping it achieve local Building and Construction Authority (BCA) approval despite its variance from normally accepted standards.

As the Skytrain approaches Jewel, passengers will have a good view of the 463kWp-rated 1,381-panel solar array that has been installed on the train station roof—one of the two arrays that have been installed as part of the Jewel project with output totalling 830kW. This makes it one of the largest solar energy arrays in Asia. With the combined energy efficiency measures and this renewable energy initiative, Jewel has achieved a Green Mark Gold+ environmental rating from the Singapore BCA.

Jewel is truly a building of today, designed using the very latest in digital modeling to predict with a high degree of certainty how its spaces will perform under all conditions. With the challenging environment of Singapore it would be unthinkable to build such a colossal public space for people and plants without having a very good idea of its comfort level. The techniques used to model and predict these conditions relied upon the physicists at Atelier Ten, a great deal of computer power, and instincts cultivated from years of experience. This is the essence of modern interactive design—instinct, analysis, and collaboration going hand in hand.

This newest generation of glasshouse advances the typology's legacy, providing optimal comfort and daylight while minimizing energy consumption through building envelope optimization, air movement, air-conditioning, energy recovery systems, and renewable energy. All while making the systems more or less disappear from view. It's a far cry from the European botanical glasshouse of the past, where the maintenance of plants was all that really mattered.

As a new centerpiece to the world's best airport, in arguably the world's greenest city, Jewel represents a huge investment in the belief that man is never happier than when he is comfortably immersed in and awed by nature. With the opening of this extraordinary building, airports will never be quite the same again.

A glass balustrade around the Rain Vortex base helps contain the dispersal of heat and humidity in its proximity

About the Contributors

Sam Lubell has written 10 books about architecture for Phaidon, Rizzoli, Metropolis Books, Monacelli Press, and Oro Editions. He writes for *The New York Times, The Los Angeles Times, Architectural Digest, Wallpaper, Dwell, Wired, The Atlantic, Metropolis, Architectural Record, The Architect's Newspaper, Architect Magazine,* and other publications. He co-curated the exhibition *Never Built New York* at the Queens Museum, and *Never Built Los Angeles* at the A+D Architecture and Design Museum.

Liew Mun Leong is Chairman of Changi Airport Group and Surbana Jurong Group, a large consultancy group in urban and infrastructure development. Mr. Liew sits on the boards of Singapore Exchange, Singapore China Foundation, and the Chinese Development Assistance Council. He also chairs the Board of Temasek Foundation Nurtures, the Management Advisory Board of NUS Business School, and the NUS School of Continuing and Lifelong Education (SCALE) Industry Advisory Board. He is a Senior International Advisor at Temasek.

Lee Seow Hiang is CEO of Changi Airport Group. He was appointed to the Board as Executive Director on June 16, 2009. Mr. Lee is Deputy Chairman of Changi Airports International, Director of Jewel Changi Airport Holding, and Chairman of the Changi Foundation Board. He holds the appointment of President of Airports Council International (ACI) Asia-Pacific Regional Board and is a member on the ACI World Governing Board. He also sits on the Board of NTUC FairPrice Co-operative and SMRT Corporation.

Moshe Safdie is an architect, urban planner, educator, theorist, and author. Embracing a comprehensive and humane design philosophy, Safdie is committed to architecture that supports and enhances a project's program; that is, informed by the geographic, social, and cultural elements that define a place, and responding to human needs and aspirations.

Over a celebrated 50-year career, Safdie has explored the essential principles of socially responsible design with a distinct visual language. His wide range of completed projects include cultural, educational, and civic institutions; neighborhoods and public parks; housing; mixed-use urban centers and airports; and master plans for existing communities and entirely new cities. Safdie's projects can be found in North and South America, and throughout Asia.

A citizen of Israel, Canada, and the United States, Safdie graduated from McGill University. In 1964 he established his own firm to realize

Habitat 67, an adaptation of his undergraduate thesis and a turning point in modern architecture. Most recently, he was awarded the Wolf Prize in Architecture for a career motivated by the social concerns of architecture and formal experimentation.

Jaron Lubin is a Principal at Safdie Architects. He has worked alongside Moshe Safdie to produce an extensive portfolio of proposals, competition entries, and realized projects, spanning a variety of geographic contexts, scales, and programs. Lubin led the design team consortium for Jewel Changi Airport, orchestrating the design competition and managing the team through design development. He was Project Architect for SkyPark at Marina Bay Sands, and has provided design leadership for the expansion of the Marina Bay Sands resort, the Sky Habitat residential tower development, and EDITION Singapore.

Charu Kokate is a Principal at Safdie Architects, Director of the Singapore office, and leader of the firm's efforts in Southeast Asia. Kokate oversaw design and construction of Singapore's Marina Bay Sands resort and Sky Habitat residential tower development. As Project Director of Jewel Changi Airport, she headed its design integration and construction. Kokate is currently supervising the design and construction of EDITION Singapore, the new Surbana Jurong Global Headquarters and District Eco-Garden in Singapore, and the Altair Residences in Colombo, Sri Lanka.

Adam Greenspan is a Directing Partner at PWP Landscape Architecture. He has been the lead designer on a wide range of projects including public parks, campuses, estates, and design competitions, among them Marina Bay Sands resort, Transbay Transit Center park in San Francisco, and Glenstone Museum and art park in Potomac, Maryland.

Cristobal Correa is Project Director at BuroHappold's New York office, leading the design of tension structures, façades, art installations, long-span structures, stadiums, and temporary buildings, as well as more traditional buildings of concrete and steel.

Craig Schwitter is a Partner at BuroHappold, founding the firm's first North American office in New York more than 20 years ago. Under his leadership, the firm has expanded to multiple cities throughout the United States and now employs nearly 240 staff regionally. Schwitter's portfolio of projects span across sectors, from cultural, higher education, and civic developments to transportation, stadia, and master-planning initiatives.

Patrick Bellew is a founding Director of Atelier Ten and has been awarded a Royal Designer of Industry in the U.K. Bellew is involved in projects across Atelier Ten's 11 worldwide offices. With extensive experience in the integration of environmental and building systems with architecture, he has particular expertise in thermal mass energy-storage technologies, environmental building design, and high-efficiency building conditioning systems.

Meredith Davey is a Director at Atelier Ten and has led a series of international projects with an emphasis on high-performance design, energy efficiency, and sustainability. Davey leads the firm's U.K. environmental design practice and building engineering teams. Alongside Jewel, notable projects include Gardens by the Bay in Singapore, Google's worldwide headquarters in California, and Google's European headquarters in London.

Henry Woon is the Director of Atelier Ten's Singapore office. He specializes in integrating computational simulation capabilities and building principles to deliver high-performance engineering solutions. Woon has led projects across the world, including Meixi Lake Sustainable Building Exhibition Centre in China and TMB Headquarters in Turkey. During the Jewel Changi construction phase, he worked closely with the design and contractor teams to ensure the incorporation of all environmental design criteria.

Martin C. Pedersen is a writer and editor based in New Orleans. He was formally executive editor at *Metropolis Magazine*. Currently he serves as executive director at Common Edge Collaborative.

Project Team

Client
Changi Airport Group
CapitaLand
Jewel Changi Airport Development

Design Architect
Safdie Architects

Executive Architect
RSP Architects

Retail Interior Design
Benoy

Design Landscape Architect
PWP Landscape Architecture

Landscape Architect
ICN Design International Pte Ltd

Water Feature Specialist
WET

Lighting Design
Lighting Planners Associates (LPA)

Design Engineer–Roof and Façades
BuroHappold

Qualified Professional/Executive Design Engineer
RSP Engineers

MEP Engineer
Mott Macdonald Singapore Pte Ltd

Building Services Engineers
Atelier Ten

Fire Safety Engineer
IGnesis

Wayfinding and Signage
Pentagram
Entro Communications

Acoustic Consultant
ARUP Acoustics

Building Maintenance
Access Advisors

Quantity Surveyor
Arcadis Singapore Pte Ltd

Main Contractor
Woh Hup
Obayashi Singapore

Illustrations and Film Work
Neoscape

Team Members

Changi Airport Group
Chairman: Liew Mun Leong
CEO: Lee Seow Hiang
Executive Vice President: Lim Peck Hoon

CapitaLand
President & GCEO: Lim Ming Yan
CEO: Lim Beng Chee
Deputy CEO: Simon Ho
President, Singapore & International: Jason Leow
Chief Retail Innovation Officer: Wilson Tan
Team
Chet Siew Chng, Jacqueline Lee, Khor Ching Wei, Kia Sing Low, Simon Yong, Tan Boon Seng

Jewel Changi Airport Development
CEO: Philip Yim / Hung Jean
Project Director: Ashith Alva
Projects Deputy Head: Philip Su
Projects: Leong Wei Hao
Team
UX: Diane Hioe, Jeremy Yeo, Koh Ji Lei
Leasing: Adeline Hong, Amanda Ong, Candy He, Cherie Chan, Cheryl Ng, Crystal Tan, Jan Tan, Jeslyn Koh, Keith Kek, Steve Chan, Tan Mui Neo, Tricia Ng, Winnie Tan, Wong Man Ling
Projects: Angeline Ang, Cheong Siew Hong, Cheng Liping, Erinna Pak, Fiona Chua, Goo Chuen Cheng, Ignatius Chin, Jocelyn Loke, Joel Sudhakar, Joyce Tan, Kelvin Wong, Khaja Nazimuddeen, Koh Lok Joon, Koh Ming Sue, Lee Xin Rui, Lim Chee Yong, Lim Teck Koon, Lim Zhi Yang, Lye Boon Kiat, Nikkole Ng, Norman Yapp, Ong Wee Boon, Samantha Lee, Shirlene Sim, Stephanie Pang, Su Huixin, Susan Tang, Tan Meiling, Yan Qingling

Safdie Architects
Lead Designer: Moshe Safdie, FAIA, FRAIC, OAA, SIA
Principals: Charu Kokate, Jaron Lubin, Greg Reaves, AIA, LEED AP
Team
Andrew Tulen, Anthony DePace, Benjy Lee, Damon Sidel, Dan Lee, David Foxe, Gary Branch, Isaac Safdie, Jack Moeller, Jeremy Schwartz, Karlo De Guzman, Marshall Peck, Peter Mark Morgan, Reihaneh Ramezany, Seunghyun Kim, Tan Lee Hua, Temple Simpson, Yinette Guzman

RSP Architects
Managing Director: Lee Kut Cheung
Project Director: Ronny Soh
Associate Directors: Chris Tan, David Tan, Nina Loo
Team
Darren Tee, Ellyn Teng, Emily Seck, Gareth Wong, Jeral Lai, Roderick Delgado, Sean Chew, Sean Mulcahy, Soon Lay Kuan, Thomas Wong

Benoy
Director: Terence Seah
Team
Clement Kho, Ernest Ng, Gina Goh, Lee Lim Qing Ping, Mark Chen, Max Chung

PWP Landscape Architecture
Partners: Peter Walker, Adam Greenspan, Julie Canter
Team
Chelsea DeWitt, Doug Findlay, Eustacia Brossart, Jennifer Corlett, Laurel Hunter, Michael Dellis

ICN Design International Pte Ltd
Managing Director: Terrence Fernando
Director: Henry Steed
Team
Carol Chuah Mei Ling, Chia Jui Siang, Tomoki Mita

WET
CEO: Mark Fuller
Project Director: Tony Freitas
Team
Tim Hunter (Senior Designer), David Duplanty (Chief Architect), Paul Woody (Architectural Designer), Sean Neprud (Project Engineer),

Jim Scheffler (Audio Systems Engineer), Steven Burkholder (Systems Integrator), Kranti Vangipuram (Controls Engineer), Gautam Rangan (Animator), Lachlan Turczan (Choreographer), Ting Zhang (Experience Visualizer), Peter Kopik (Director of Design), Jose Aleman (Field Technician), Chuck Schmitz (Manager, Mock-up and Testing)

Lighting Planners Associates (LPA)
Principal: Kaoru Mende
Team
Gaurav Jain, Hattori Yusuke, Niken Wulandari,
Phraporn Kasemtavornsilpa, Ryan Valentino, Shunichi Ikeda,
Sunyoung Hwang

BuroHappold
Partner: Craig Schwitter
Project Directors: Cristobal Correa, Hormoz Houshmand
Team
Alexandra Vlasova, Chandra Dinata, Georgios Papadogeorgakis,
Gustav Fagerstrom, Jeff Thompson, John Ivanoff, Katherine Chan,
Liam McNamara, Rachel Shillander, Roger Liu, Shrikant Sharma,
Trevor Stephen Lewis, Whitney Lee

RSP Engineers
Managing Director: Lai Huen Poh
Team
Anthony Tan, Edwin Ong, Ho Peir Meng, Jessica Lim, Lai Chung Hee,
Nathanael Yong

Mott Macdonald Singapore Pte Ltd
Project Director: Tan Chee Chuan
Project Manager: Ong Thiam Guan
Technical Director: Soh Kai Yea
Team
Jade Bai, Koh Pei Xin, Lim Wi Hong, Sandy Lim, Welmina Chua,
Xu Wei Wei

Atelier Ten
Directors: Patrick Bellew, Meredith Davey, Henry Woon
Team
Ace Glen Garcia, Ajay Shah, Chris Killoran, Corinna Gage,
James Sheldon, Nikolai Artmann, Reinier Zeldenrust, Seohaa Choi,
Tilly Lenartowicz

IGnesis
Director: Henry Ho
Team
Ang Shue Ni, Toh Yun Ying, Wong Yin Ying

Pentagram
Michael Gericke, Don Bilodeau, Jed Skillins

Entro Communications
Anthony Chua, Gordon McTaggart, Raymond Cheung, Wayne McCutcheon

ARUP Acoustics
Alban Bassuet, Clemeth Abercrombie, Jingfeng Xu, Nick Boulter

Arcadis Singapore Pte Ltd
Director: Seah Choo Meng
Senior Director: Tricia Tang
Team
Chloe Foo, Ho Kong Mo, Hong Koh Tee, Jason Ling, Josephine Lee, Tim Risbridger

Woh Hup
Chairman: Yong Nam Seng
Deputy Chairman: Yong Tiam Yoon
Executive Directors: Neil Yong, Yong Derong, Ngiam Siew Kim
Project Director: Ng Yew Hung
Deputy Project Director: G. Gunasekaran
Team
Goh Hock Jin (Senior Site Manager), Chai Koh Fong (Senior Site Manager), Cao Bao Chun (Site Manager), Han Kong Juan (Site Manager), Stella Chung (Contracts Manager), Andrew Neo (M&E Manager), Cong Zhengxia (Technical Manager), Wong Keam Tong (Engineering Director), Tan Beng Chwee (M&E Director), Loo Eng Teck (Senior Contracts Manager), Selvamani Murugappan (QAQC Manager), Ong Chin Chong (Architecture Manager)

Obayashi Singapore
Managing Director: Lee Aik Seng
Executive Directors: Jun Narasaka, Atsushi Nakagawa
Deputy Project Director: Hidefumi Sakurai

Team
Yoshiyuki Tsutsui (Construction Manager), Yeo Ek Eng Ivan (M&E Manager), Sun Yuezhen (Design Manager), Ho Peck (Contract Manager), Ng Siew Loong (BIM Manager), Natarajan Kannan (Site Manager), Yong Jyh Yih (Construction Manager), Lee Boon Hock (Site Manager), Koh Keng Hock (Site Manager)

Subcontractors
Alto (Interior Ambient Lighting), Alucobond (Metal Panels), B&B Italia (Tables), Bega (Pole Light and Footlight), Benaire Engineering Pte Ltd (Floor grille), Bosch (Public Address & EVC Systems), Briton (Hardware), Chien Noir Sarl (Jumping Nets), Choon Hin Stainless Steel Pte Ltd (Façade), CLF Shutters Asia Pte Ltd (Security Grilles), Colt Louvres (Louvered Panels), CoxGomyl (Building Maintenance), CSG Holding (Glass Panels), Deshin Engineering & Construction Pte Ltd (Metalwork), Designbythem (Chairs), Dormakaba (Sliding Doors), DSG Projects Singapore Pte Ltd (Yotel ID Works), Exploratorium (Exhibition Provided), Elmes (Hardware), Endo (Interior Ambient Lighting), Etesse Carpets (Carpet), Fast Flow Singapore Pte Ltd (Rainwater Downpipe), Fitz Hansen (Chairs), Flamelite (S) Pte Ltd (Linkbridge Glass Doors), Formica (Plastic Laminate Interior Finishes) ,Fuji Signcrafts Industries Pte Ltd (Signage), GB Irrigation Pte Ltd (Irrigation System), GNT Glass Co Ltd (Canopy Bridge Glass Flooring), Guthrie Engineering (S) Pte Ltd (ACMV System), +Halle (Chairs), Hart Engineering (Engineered Smoke Control), Hi! Services Industries Pte Ltd (Metalworks), Hitachi Aqua-Tech Engineering Pte Ltd (Water Feature), HK lighting (Tree Uplight and External Lighting), Hwaco Steel (Canopy Bridge Stainless Steel Cladding), iDAS Technology (Engineered Smoke Control), Imperfecto Lab (Chairs), King Wan Construction Pte Ltd (Plumbing & Sanitary Works), KKDC (Trail Coping Footlight), Kvadrat (Upholstery), LG Hi-Macs(Interior Finishes Solid Surfacing), LHL International Pte Ltd (Enclosure to Link Bridges, Glass Lifts and Changi Airport Skytrain System), LNT Coating (ETFE Steel Work), Lumenpulse (Façade External Lighting), Lutron (Lighting Control System), Macalloy (Canopy Bridge Cables), Maerich (Canopy Bridge Lighting), Marquis in collaboration with Nathan Yong (Chairs), Mero Asia Pacific Pte Ltd (Roof Façade), Metalix (Staircases), Meyer (Inground Tree Uplight), M&G Contracts (Lavastone Tiles), Milliken & Company (Carpet), Muuto (Tables), Officium (Walking Nets), Panframe (Acoustic Ceiling), Passage Projects (ETFE System and Canopy Bridge), Porada (Tables), Prime Structures Engineering Pte Ltd (Design and Built Canopy Bridge), Reynolds Polymer Technology (Acrylic Rain Vortex), Roblon (Fiber Optics), Rockfon (Acoustical Ceilings),

Subcontractors Continued

Ronstan International (Canopy Cables), Schindler Lifts (Singapore) Pte Ltd (Lift, Escalators and Travellators), Shinryo Singapore Pte Ltd (Air-conditioning & M/V), SolarGy Pte Ltd (Photovoltaic System), Sprinkler Engineering (Fire Protection Systems), Sunray Woodcraft Construction Pte Ltd (ID Work in Common Areas), Synthesis (Aluminum Panels), Tacam Steel Pte Ltd (Metal Doors), Technolite (Singapore) Pte Ltd in collaboration with Futuro Luce (Design, Supply, Delivery of Architectural Light Fittings), TEHC International Pte Ltd (Softscape), TET Engineering and Metalworks (ETFE System), Tokistar (Interior Retail Covelight and Catenary Lighting), Topmast Engineering Pte Ltd (Hoarding T1E), Tractel Singapore Pte ltd (BMU for Link Bridge), UG M&E Pte Ltd (Electrical), Ushio Asia Pacific (Growlight System), Valoya (Growlight System), Vector Foiltec Pte Ltd (ETFE System), Venturer Pte Ltd (Timber Decking), Vitra (Reception Furniture), Vitro Architectural Glass (Glass Panels), We-ef (Event Space and External Lighting), Won-Door (Fire-control Doors), YJ International (Interior Roller Shades), Yongnam Engineering & Construction (Pte) Ltd (Steel Structure Work), Zumtobel (Downlight External Lighting)

Neoscape

Carlos Cristerna, Dan Ferraro, Dave Parmenter, Jason Addy, Jerry Chen, Vasilli Shields

Illustration Credits

Atelier Ten
148 (all)

BuroHappold
139, 140 (all), 142 (all), 100 (bottom left)

Changi Airport Group
19

Darren Soh
12/13, 38/39, 53, 55, 72, 74/75, 78/79, 86, 88, 89, 90/91, 102/103, 104/105, 106/107, 108/109, 110/111, 112/113, 114/115, 116/117, 118/119, 128, 136, 137, 150/151, back cover

Full Bleed Pte Ltd.
Front cover

Hong Ray Photography
101 (left)

Matthew Pillsbury
95

Neoscape
24/25, 34/35

PWP Landscape Architecture
132 (all), 134 (all)

Ronnie Soh
143

Safdie Architects
20/21, 28, 29, 30, 32/33, 52, 59, 60, 65, 66, 67, 73, 80 (bottom right), 100 (center right & bottom center), 122 (all), 123 (all but center), 125, 126, 129, 144/145, 147

Timothy Hursley
4/5, 40/41, 43, 44, 46, 47, 48, 51, 54, 56, 57, 58, 61, 62/63, 68/69, 70, 71, 76/77, 82/83, 84/85, 87, 99

WET
123 (center)

Reference Imagery

16/17

Overview of Terminal 1 in the Evening (2012), Creative Commons

27

(top left) *The Garden of Eden* (1610–12), Museum: Thyssen-Bornemisza Collections, Bruegel the Elder, Jan/Alamy Stock Photo; (top right) *Hanging Gardens of Babylon* (16th century), Martin Heemskerck/Alamy Stock Photo; (center left) *Ancient Wonder of the World, Gardens of Babylon*, Science History Images/Alamy Stock Photo; (bottom left) A part of Giant Traditional Chinese Painting (2006), Mr. Chen Minglou/Creative Commons Compatible License; (bottom center) *Wonders of the Ancient World* (19th century), World History Archive/Alamy Stock Photo; (bottom right) *The Tower of Babel* (1563), Pieter Bruegel the Elder, Dutch School/Alamy Stock Photo

96

(left) *Expo 67 in Montreal Quebec* (1967), Canada Bill Engdahl/Library of Congress Prints and Photographs Division; (right) *Trans World Airlines Terminal, John F. Kennedy (originally Idlewild) Airport, New York, New York, 1956–62 Information Desk* Balthazar Korab / Library of Congress Prints and Photographs Division

131

Mist, over tropical rainforest, early morning, Sabah, Borneo, Malaysia (2015), Jon Arnold Images Ltd / Alamy Stock Photo

Instagram

80

(top left) Zipeng Lee @zippyzipeng; (top center) @seekuan_sk; (top right) Vivian Nguyen @viviannguyen8x; (bottom left) Susan Koh @ajugglingmom; (center right) Ivanna Megdalena @ivannamagdalena

81

(top left) Madeni Jais @muddyknee; (top right) @dionisiusnio; (center left) Kelvin Ang @cheekiemonkies; (bottom left) Zipeng Lee @zippyzipeng; (bottom center) Ivan Kuek @phonenomenon; (bottom right) @changiairport

100

(top left) i-Weekly @iweeklymag; (top center) Nola Baldy @riafinola; (top right) @avril_24; (center left) @choypeng-chong; (center) Takashi Murakami @takashipom; (bottom right) @taramilktea

101

(top right) @a-hugomarc; (bottom right) @yoga3ozquin

Acknowledgments

The creation of Jewel Changi Airport is the result of the leadership and vision of Changi Airport Group in collaboration with CapitaLand. We are grateful to the dedicated team at Jewel Changi Airport Development who worked tirelessly to realize this vision.
Thank you to all the team members who have contributed their efforts to the success of the project, the multitude of which would be impossible to list in its entirety.
All efforts have been made to trace original source material. Special thanks to Michael Gericke, Matt McInerney, Tess Beckingham, and Natalie Wanjek in the production of this publication.